NATIONALIZATION

NATIONALIZATION

A STUDY IN THE PROTECTION OF ALIEN PROPERTY IN INTERNATIONAL LAW

by

ISI FOIGHEL

ASSISTANT PROFESSOR IN THE UNIVERSITY OF COPENHAGEN
ATTORNEY-AT-LAW

GREENWOOD PRESS, PUBLISHERS
WESTPORT, CONNECTICUT

Library of Congress Cataloging in Publication Data

Foighel, Isi, 1927-
Nationalization : a study in the protection of alien property in international law.

"Reprint from Acta Scandinavica juris centium [i.e. gentium]"--P.
Reprint. Originally published: London : Stevens ; Copenhagen : Nyt nordisk forlag, 1957.
Bibliography: p.
Includes index.
1. Eminent domain (International law)
2. Alien property. I. Title.
JX4263.P6F6 1982 341.4'8 82-6263
ISBN 0-8371-7675-1 (lib. bdg.) AACR2

Reprinted by arrangement with Sweet & Maxwell, Ltd.

Reprinted in 1982 by Greenwood Press
A division of Congressional Information Service, Inc.
88 Post Road West, Westport, Connecticut 06881

Printed in the United States of America

10 9 8 7 6 5 4 3 2 1

THE QUESTION of the international concequences of nationalization has got into the focus of the evolution of international law. The nationalization of the Suez Maritime Canal Company is only the last of a number of interferences with property which have attracted the attention of public world opinion and given rise to farreaching complications. In the discussion of this problem the classical principles of European international law, based on the philosophy of liberalism and private capitalism, are wrestling with new points of view born of a different political and economic ideology. Strong nationalistic tendencies, too, have marked the theory and practice in the new states that have been liberated from the dependency of former days. Eager to realize fully the newborn independence, they want to free themselves of the bonds of foreign capital representing in their eyes colonialism and imperialism, and demonstrate their ability to utilize their resources independently. These new nations, earlier without a voice in the international society, now, as members of the United Nations on a equal footing with others, have gained a possibility of influencing the evolution of international law.

The classical principles of adequate, prompt and effective compensation for deprivation of property have met not only ideological opposition but also technical obstacles. The extensive nationalizations, comprising, not the property of a single individual, but whole sectors of the economic system of the country, of necessity must give rise to problems which cannot technically be solved on the basis of a few simple principles. In such cases the general rules of international law have given way to specific treaty arrangements in which a global account between the states has superseded individual settlements with the claimants concerned.

Only the future may show what will be the outcome of the conflicting ideas and forces. Perhaps the classical ideas possess greater vital force than some are inclined to believe. Perhaps the new nations some day will realize that there is an inconsistency between their need for investment of foreign capital and an ideology and policy discouraging such investment and increasing the price of it.

In this book, Isi Foighel, Assistant Professor in the University of Copenhagen, has collected a comprehensive material suited to elucidate this problem. I want especially to point to the many treaties and national enactments which have been compiled and analyzed instructively, presenting the reader with a body of information not to be found elsewhere in legal literature. I am convinced that this book will contribute to clarify the discussion and I take pleasure in commending it as an interesting study of one of the most ardent problems of modern international law.

Copenhagen, August 1957.

ALF ROSS, L. L. D., Ph. D.
Professor in the University
of Copenhagen.

CONTENTS

PART I: BACKGROUND

PART II: LEGALITY

PART III: COMPENSATION

PART I: BACKGROUND

§ 1.
INTRODUCTION(1)

On 13th February, 1918, immediately after the new régime in Soviet Russia had issued decrees concerning the nationalization of all large industrial and banking undertakings, the United States ambassador in Petrograd handed the Government of Soviet Russia a Note of protest which declared:

> "In order to avoid any misunderstandings in the future, the representatives at Petrograd of all the foreign Powers declare that they view the decrees relating to ... the confiscation of property and other similar measures as null and void in so far as their nationals are concerned."

Thirty-eight years after the handing over of this Note, on 26th July, 1956, the Egyptian dictator, Colonel Nasser, proclaimed the nationalization of the Suez Canal. This nationalization, too, was met with protests on the part of practically speaking the same States as were represented in Petrograd on the earlier occasion, but these protests were of a completely different character and quite different

---

(1) — This treatise was submitted in the price competition of the University of Copenhagen 1955 and in 1956 the author was awarded the Gold Medal of the University. The treatise is published in essentially the same form in which it was submitted to adjudication. A few sections have been left out and the situation existing at the time of publishing has caused a few additions to be made.

The treatise has been translated from the Danish by *Mrs. Margaret Dutton. Mr. Ralph Bentsen,* Attorney-at-Law and sworn Interpreter and Translator of the English language, has given valuable assistance in the solution of many of the problems of juridico-linguistic nature involved.

For economic assistance to carry through and publish this work the author conveys thanks to the *General Scientific Fund of the Danish State* and the *Rask-Ørsted Foundation* and *Acta Scandinavica Juris Gentium.*

substance. This is shown clearly in the reactions of those States which were invited to take part in the first London Conference in August 1956 to consider the situation in Egypt. Only a very few of these countries protested against the nationalization as such, whilst the overwhelming majority on the other hand declared that the nationalization was an outcome of Egypt's legitimate rights. Apparently none of the countries was minded to declare that a nationalization of foreign property situated in Egypt was in itself in breach of international law, still less that the Egyptian measures were regarded as null and void in so far as foreign nationals and interests were concerned.

The difference in reaction to these two cases of nationalization opens up a field of vision that is not without interest. It may be reasonable to assume that the difference is not — or at least not solely — motivated by the fact that the Egyptian nationalization took place in a domain where the political situation required the Western Powers to exercise the greatest care to avoid any political or strategic error whereby they might forfeit possible sympathy and influence in favour of the Eastern group of Powers. The reaction to an act of nationalization is not so simple and uncomplicated that it can be explained merely by a reference to the standing conflict between East and West.

The motivation of the difference must rather be looked for in the development in the realm of politics and economics and as a consequence also in international law that has taken place in the period between the two nationalizations.

Up till 1918 the conception of international law concerning the protection of foreign property was determined in particularly by the fact that those countries which were the object for foreign investments were widely trusted. Economically, the countries that were members of the family of nations were liberal, and their political systems of such a character that expropriation in respect of foreigners occurred but rarely. The international legal view was — and it could not be otherwise — determined by the time-honoured liberal dogma of the inviolability of property.

This fundamental basis of the international legal view no longer exists. The family of nations has been widened to include a considerable number of countries whose influence upon the development of international law cannot be dismissed. New economic systems have seen the light, and a great number of the members of the family of nations are now adherents of ideologies which, as compared with the Liberal view, represent an entire revaluation of the relationship between the individual and the state, and of the fundamental concepts of Liberalism, including in particular that of property.

As a result, the problems of the legal protection of alien property are at the present time undergoing an evolution, as yet hardly fully clarified, though it is possible to indicate tendencies and views which may be taken to show the direction it is following. This evolution is of vital importance not only for that group of private persons or companies which hold property in countries where nationalization has taken place, or is likely to take place, but also particularly for those countries which formally and materially are described as underdeveloped, and whose reconstruction and development necessitates extensive investments on the part of countries richer in capital. In these two fields — private investment in foreign countries and the United Nations' programme for technical assistance to underdeveloped countries — the rules of international law concerning the protection of alien property against nationalization raise legal and political problems of vital international importance.

It is these problems and the evolution which has taken place in this field of law in recent decades that are the subject of the following study.

§ 2.
WHAT IS NATIONALIZATION?

If we wish to pick out one single feature of the social-economic character of the 20th century, one fact accompanying the technical development will strike us very forcibly: the direct and indirect interference by government action with private property. The Declaration of the Rights of Man of 1789, describing ownership as one of the natural and inalienable human rights, has long since been of exclusively historical interest. And when the sanctity of ownership is laid down even in the most modern constitutions, it is at the same time also generally recognized that such provisions are without practical juridical relevance(1).

The individual citizen in olden times could only be made to relinquish his property in return for complete and prompt compensation,

(1) Cf. in the case of Danish Law: Alf Ross and Ernst Andersen, *Dansk Statsforfatningsret* II, (1948), p. 212, Poul Andersen, *Dansk Statsforfatningsret I*, (1954), p. 719. cf. Egon Larsen, *Tvungen Ejendomsafståelse*, (1940), p. 60.

but nowadays private ownership has gradually — in the interests of the community — been more and more undermined. Thus in the power of the state to impose general restrictions on property (social restrictions, building laws, santation laws etc.) there is authority for public interference with property, which can be just as serious for the indvidual as expropriation in the traditional narrow sense, but without creating any claim for compensation.

Public interference with property, however, in the period of the Russian revolution, apparently took new forms; in many countries there was, to a varying extent, interference with property of an at any rate unorthodox nature, viz., nationalization.

This new form of public acquisition of private property for the benefit of the common good necessitates an examination firstly of the question whether there is a difference between nationalization and expropriation in traditional sense, and secondly whether if a difference can be found it has legal relevance, such that a distinction between nationalization and other forms of public interference with property may be upheld.

A. *Is there a difference of fact between nationalization and other forms of public interference with property?*

1. *The traditional view.* It is possible in the theory and practice of international law to find agreement as to the characteristic of the concept of expropriation in traditional sense, namely, a compulsory acquisition of property which takes place for the benefit of the common good and which gives to the person affected by the expropriation a claim to full compensation. However, there exists no such agreement among the writers who have studied the international problems of nationalization. The majority of these writers seem to have been dazzled by the new political and economic policy which has led to nationalization and have simply assumed that what the individual states describe as nationalization is also and exclusively nationalization as understood in international law, and on this basis attempts have then been made to state special rules of international law without first deciding whether nationalization — apart from the political and economic background — differs from previously known forms of public acquisition of property, or at any rate without determining clearly what the difference is.

These writers define nationalization as a public acquisition of property for the benefit of the common good, and differing from the traditional forms, expropriation and general restrictions on property in one or more of the following points:

motive
purpose
extent
subject-matter and/or
form.

A few examples may be mentioned:

As the starting point and basis for discussion in the unfinished debate on the international effects of nationalization, held in 1952 at the Institut de Droit Internationale, *La Pradelle*(1) defined nationalization as:

> "... opération de haute politique par laquelle un Etat réformant tout ou partie de sa structure économique enlève aux personnes privées pour la remettre à la nation la disposition d'entreprises industrielles ou agricoles d'une certaine importance en les faisant passer du secteur privé au secteur public."

By this definition La Pradelle appears — and this also appears from the debate — to attach decisive importance to the *motive* for the public interference with property, and in his definition of the concept(2) presupposes in addition that nationalization differs from expropriation in that this latter is of only local importance, whereas nationalization is motivated by a complete and general change of policy.

By reason of its indefinite terms and its unsuitability as a basis for distinction(3) La Pradelle's definition gave rise to lengthy debate, at the conclusion of which the Institute adopted the following definition(4):

> "La nationalization est le transfert à l'Etat, par mesure législative et dans un intérêt public, de biens ou droits privés d'une certaine catégorie, en vue de leur exploitation ou contrôle par l'Etat, ou d'une nouvelle destination qui leur serait donnée par celui-ci."

In this definition the Institute abandoned the juridically vague statement of motive as the relevant fact and attached the concept of nationalization to the *purpose* of the expropriation.

As an example of the group of writers who attach decisive importance to the *extent* of the public interference with property *Fried-*

(1) *Annuaire*, vol. 43 I, (1950), p. 126.
(2) *op. cit.*, p. 128.
(3) Cf. *infra*.
(4) *Annuaire*, vol. 44 II, (1952), p. 283.

man(1) may by quoted; he does not think it a conceptual necessity that the nationalization measures encroach upon the economic structure of the community, since nationalization does not prevent the retention of private capital, and can indeed provide occasion for a certain co-operation between private interests and state capital, for nationalization only needs to exclude private capital in so far as concerns the property itself in nationalized undertakings. Friedman sees nationalization as a special form of expropriation, namely as a deprivation of property, general and determined by kind, for the benefit of the common good.

Doman(2) defines nationalization as a more or less extensive general impersonal intervention in the economic structure — in the best interests of the nation — with or without compensation. Where compensation is paid, then, according to this author, it is a case of expropriation. Where there is no compensation it is a case of confiscation.

According to this definition, nationalization is no new concept, but a superterm for any other forms of public interference with property.

Finally, as an example of a writer who in his definition of the concept attaches weight to form, motive, extent, subject-matter, as to purpose, there may be mentioned *Rolin*(3), who puts forward the following definition:

> "La nationalisation est la mesure législative de caractère politique par laquelle un Etat, réformant la structure de son économie, enlève aux personnes privées et confie à des organismes publics la jouissance et l'administration d'entreprises industrielles ou agricoles de nature déterminée."

2. *Critical valuation.* The present study does not necessitate a detailed criticism of the views quoted, but in general the following remarks may be made:

To establish the *motive* for an act of the state can in practice present difficulty(4), and in particular a court would find it hard to set aside an assertion put forward by a state to the effect that this or that motive had been the decisive factor. Nevertheless the introduction of the motive for an action into the definition of the same can have a certain significance, namely as a negative criterion

(1) *Expropriation in International Law,* (1953), p. 12.

(2) *Postwar Nationalization of Foreign Property in Europe,* Columbia Law Review, vol. 48, (1948), p. 1125.

(3) *Annuaire,* vol. 43 I, (1950), p. 99.

(4) Cf. Fischer-Williams, *International Law and the Property of Aliens,* BYIL, vol. 9, (1928), p. 26.

in the sense that those circumstances at any rate must be excluded from the domain of the definition which are clearly not the outcome of the particular motive. It is, however, a natural prerequisite that a statement of motive must have a certain solidity and clarity to be practicable. Thus if in the definition of nationalization it is stated that the intervention must be a part of the alteration of the economic structure of the state and thus be dictated by motives of social economics, then it is possible to abstract from the domain of the definition acts of public interference with property of the nature of penal, health, security or police measures, but the closer demarcation, for example, between nationalization and expropriation, does not appear possible on the basis of a criterion like this.

Nor does the *extent* of the intervention seem to provide the necessary clarity and solidity as a criterion for a distinction between certain public acquisitions of property. But here it must be remembered that even if it is typical that the intervention of nationalization is general, i. e. covers all property of the same kind, for example, all industrial undertakings of a certain size or all banks, it is nevertheless not expedient in the definition of the term to talk exclusively of nationalization when this condition is fulfilled. The French Nationalization Law of 2nd December, 1945, thus covered only(1) the Banque de France and the four largest commercial banks, and not other important banking enterprises. It seems definitely inexpedient not to consider the French nationalization law as giving warrant for nationalization in the sense understood in international law.

On the other hand many cases of public interferences with property are of a general nature without being any question of nationalization. This shows clearly that the criteria of extent alone cannot be employed as a part of the definition of nationalization as distinct from expropriation in the traditional sence.

It does occasionally happen that the criterion of *subject-matter* is used as the basis of a distinction between nationalization and expropriation. Against this it must be maintained that any property that can be expropriated can also be nationalized, and vice versa.

Whether the public acquisition of property takes place in a special *form*, for example, by enactment or by an administrative act, must as far as international law is concerned be completely irrelevant. This question only concerns those organs of state which undertake the intervention. It is quite another matter that the illegality of the act according to the national law can influence the judgement of inter-

(1) Margaret G. Meyers, *The Nationalization of Banks in France*, Political Science Quarterly, (1949), p. 189.

national law(1), but this is true equally whether it is a question of expropriation or of nationalization.

Nor can it be admitted that previous definitions which define nationalization according to the *purpose* of the interference can be used as a basis for a distinction.

Although l'Institut de Droit International has the right idea, the definition of purpose which it gives, namely "the future use and control by the state of the property taken over or its utilization for a new purpose to be determined by the state", is too comprehensive. It would be hard to find an expropriation in the traditional sense which could not equally be covered by the definition of nationalization adopted by the Institute, since all expropriated property is used by the state or utilized for another purpose determined by the state.

It appears therefore that it has not been possible among the definitions so far produced to find an expedient solution of the problem of demarcation between nationalization and other forms of public interference with property for the benefit of the common good. This might lead one to think that there is no crucial difference between nationalization and, for example, expropriation, and that nationalization is in consequence no more than a neologism motivated by modern political theories, since the very sound of words such as "the transfer of property to the common ownership of the nation" have a certain value as political slogans.

However, this is not so.

Nationalization is a special category of acquisition of property, distinguished in particular by the fact that the arguments underlying the interventions of nationalization and its purpose are quite other than those in the case of traditional forms of acquisition of property. Unlike expropriations and general restrictions on property the interventions of nationalization are not motivated by the desire of the state to take over or restrict the use of the property for the benefit of a special purpose of the state — different from the previous use; for example, expropriation of agricultural land for the purpose of laying railways and building hospitals or the restriction of building rights for the purpose of creating new roads; nationalization must seek its supporting arguments in the very circumstance *that the state does not desire to let private individuals utilize the*

(1) Cf. in this connection the *Walter Fletcher Smith Case*, (1929), which was settled by arbitration between the United States and Cuba. The expropriation here was not in conformity with the internal law, which involved liability, *A. J. I. L.*, vol. 24, (1930), p. 384.

property for so called private economic purposes, and therefore desires to take over, and carry on the hitherto practised utilization of the property.

Thus whilst in the case of expropriation in traditional sense the public authorities must undertake to weigh up the different *kinds* of utilization of the particular property, i. e. the previous utilization of the property and the future utilization that is different, the problem in the case of nationalization is another one, since the private and the state utilization of the property is of the same kind, but the distribution of the profit on the other hand is different. The problem which is solved by the relinquishing of the property and called nationalization is thus first and foremost a problem of distribution.

This is the political reality which explains the rise of nationalization and its frequent adoption in national communities built upon socialistic theories, just as the justification of the existence of the term nationalization alongside expropriation in traditional sense must on this view appear evident.

Against this background then, nationalization may be defined as *the compulsory transfer to the state of private property dictated by economic motives and having as its purpose the continued and essentially unaltered exploitation of the particular property.*

It is assumed here that the concept of nationalization does not only comprise the fact that the state carries on the former economic utilization of the property, but also the fact that in other ways the state utilizes the opportunities created by the former undertaking, for example, by the setting up of a state monopoly.

Whether the future administration of the nationalized property is carried out directly by an organ of the government, or indirectly by the establishment of a statecontrolled company to exploit the property, is of no importance. If, however, the surrendered property is transferred to private persons, then it is not a case of nationalization — cf. also ordinary linguistic usage. This was in fact the case with the so called Mexican agricultural expropriations in 1938, where among other things American agricultural holdings were parcelled out for the benefit of Mexican smallholders, and it was also the case with the Guatemala Law of 19th June, 1952, concerning the expropriation of large estates belonging to the American company, United Fruit Company(1).

---

(1) Cf. *Dep. St. Bul.*, vol. 29, (1953), p. 357 ff. Cf. also the Danish Law No. 179 of 30th March 1943 concerning the obtaining of fuel in Denmark, § 2, where

If the definition is restricted to cover only those measures which are dictated by economic motives, then other public acquisition of property is excluded from the term nationalization, inter alia, that carried out as a security measure, for example, the confiscation of undertakings with a view to war, penal confiscation(1), or measures to protect health or morality such as, for example, the establishment of a monopoly of alcohol or of a lottery. It is reasonable to suppose that this restriction is expedient, since motives other than those of social policy underly such interferences, and it may thus be presumed that there are special rules to cover such special interferences with private property.

3. *The relation between expropriation and nationalization.* Finally, it must be pointed out that the definition given here looks on nationalization as a co-ordinate term alongside expropriation and general restrictions on property.

Some writers(2), however, so understand the relationship between the various forms of interference with private property that expropriation is a special form of nationalization, whereas others(3) conversely regard nationalization as a special form of expropriation.

In assessing these constructions it must not, however, be forgotten that the framing of a legal conception as a working hypothesis exclusively is a question of expediency. So that when this study takes as its basis the view that expropriation and nationalization are co-ordinate terms, this is done chiefly because nationalization is an interference with private property of such a particular kind that an analysis of the international effects of nationalization seems to demand independent investigations without any — at best superfluous — deductions from the obscure rules of international law concerning expropriation.

---

it is thus not a case of nationalization to the extent that the surrender of the property takes place for the benefit of private individuals.

(1) Cf. Danish Law Nr. 132 of 30th March 1946 concerning the confiscation of German and Japanese property, and the French Law of 29th May 1945 concerning the transfer of the Renault works to state ownership.

(2) Doman, *op. cit.*, p. 1125 and Fawcet, *Some Foreign Effects of Nationalization of Property*, BYIL, vol. 27, (1950), p. 355.

(3) Including Friedman, *op. cit.*, p. 12 and Ross, *Annuaire*, vol. 44 II, (1952), p. 261.

B. *Is the difference of fact between nationalization and other forms of public interference with property of any relevance in international law?*

After the factual delimitation of the concept of nationalization there arises the question of whether there is a difference between nationalization and other forms of public interference with property such as to warrant a distinction as regards the law — on account of the rules of international law.

Fitzmaurice(1) takes the view that the distinction between expropriation and nationalization is a distinction of fact and without legal relevance. Between these terms there is possibly a difference of degree, method or motive, but this difference is not decisive. The result in both cases is the same(2). The person who is affected by the intervention loses his property.

As against this, *Castberg*(3) states that in the case of nationalization (in contradistinction to expropriation) there will often not even in the municipal law be a remedy for the foreigner to obtain redress; and *La Pradelle*(4) stresses the fact that nationalization (in contradistinction to expropriation) will frequently be of such wide extent that the payment of compensation to those affected would simply be an economic impossibility.

Even if the differences stressed by Castberg and La Pradelle are only typical and in any case not essential to the concept, it must however be accepted that the view communicated by Fitzmaurice is wrong, not only as to the result (cf. further Parts II and III infra), but equally in its fundamental attitude, which appears to rest upon an erroneous view of those factors which determine the substance of international law.

The fact that the individual is hit equally hard by expropriation and nationalization is irrelevant from the point of view of international law. International law is that body of rules which govern states (autonomous communities) in their mutual relations. The interests which the legal system of international law aims at protecting are those of the states, i. e. the interests of the collectivities. The way in which the single individual is treated is in principle a matter of indifference to international law, since international law is only concerned with the individual in his capacity of member

---

(1) *Annuaire*, vol. 44 II, (1952), p. 255.
(2) Cf. also Fischer-Williams, *op. cit.*, p. 25.
(3) *Annuaire*, vol. 44 II, (1952), p. 264.
(4) *Annuaire*, vol. 43 I, (1950), p. 118 and vol. 44 II, (1952), p. 254.

of a collective (a state) which has acquired particular rights. This is clear both from the international law of treaties as well as from the international customary law.

That treaties exclusively concern the interests of the state follows from the fact that in entering into a treaty a state must protect the interests of the whole country, even though this may be at the expense of individual citizens. Treaties must therefore be interpreted according to their effects for the state as a collective and not according to the effect the treaties might have with regard to the concrete interests of a citizen. The legal position of an individual as the result of a treaty must be understood as deriving from the position accorded to the collective to which he belongs(1).

The same views must be decisive for the content and understanding of the international customary law. Only thus is it possible, for example, to explain why traditional international law requires that a state shall pay compensation for the expropriation of foreign property, while this duty of compensation is not imposed upon a state that imposes heavy taxation on aliens. The interests of the individual are in both cases the same, namely, the preservation of property, while the interests of the states with regard to taxation are different from their interests with regard to expropriation. Similarly it is only by an appreciation of the interest of the collective that it is possible to explain why a former exterritorial person can be proceeded against in the courts for acts committed while he was an exterritorial(2). The interests of the particular individual are the same before and after the end of his exterritoriality, namely, to escape a penalty. The interest of the home state however are different in the two situations.

In this connection it can in addition be stated that in prevailing international law the individual cannot bring an action at law(3), but that this is left to the state to which the individual belongs, and since the question of the international upholding of the law is

---

(1) Cf. *The North Atlantic Coast Fisheries* (1910): "The inhabitants of the United States do not derive the liberty to take fish directly from the treaty but from the United States government as party to the treaty with Great Britain and moreover exercising the right to regulate the conditions under which its inhabitants may enjoy the granted liberty." (*The Permanent Court of Arbitration.* VII, p. 131).

(2) Ross, *Textbook of International Law,* (1946), p. 110: mentions the law of aliens as an example to show that the individual is the direct subject of rights (subject of interest) in international law.

(3) Cf. Ross, *loc. cit.*

exclusively determined by collective interests(1) it follows that also the substance of the rules of international law will be determined by these same interests.

Without going any further into the question of the legal status of the individual in international law, it must be possible against the background of what has been stated here to maintain that it is not a necessary conclusion that the rules of international law are homogeneous because the circumstances which the rules regulate put the individual into the same position, nor is it always true that the rules of international law are different in situations where the single individual is treated in a variety of ways. The only decisive thing is how the situation affects the interest of the state, i.e. the collective interest.

Applied to the problem before us, then, the result is that a distinction between nationalization and other forms of public interference with property may be taken to be relevant to international law, if only because the interests of the states in nationalization by reason of difference of motive and purpose, and by reason of the general very wide extent(2) of the interventions of nationalization, diverge from the state interests that are behind the other forms of public interference with property.

The correctness of this assumption will be tested further in the following chapters.

§ 3.
WHAT INTERESTS PROVIDE THE MOTIVE FOR NATIONALIZATION?

It is a typical feature of economic-political evolution that great political events, revolutions or wars, give rise to economic-social reforms, since it often happens that on the conclusion of these events

(1) Cf. Borchard, *Diplomatic Protection*, (1916), p. 351: "Factors which enter into consideration in determining the state's interposition are the seriousness of the offence, the indignity to the nation, and the political expediency of regarding the private injury as a public wrong be repaired by national action — in short, the interest of the people as a whole as against those of the citizen receive first consideration before state action is initiated."

(2) Cf. Rubin, *Nationalization and Compensation*, University of Chicago Law Review, vol. 17, (1949—50), p. 460, and Scelle, *Annuaire*, vol. 44 II, (1952), p. 267.

the people expect a change in the social order(1). Another typical feature is that these economic and social reforms involve a decision of attitude to the question of public versus private ownership, not only because the state has to procure the means for its programme of reform, but because the very possession of property and in particular ownership and control of the large industrial undertakings in a country are closely connected with the question of power.

A closer analysis of the motives behind the moves to nationalize, however, shows that there are a number of different groups of factors that play a part here.

An understanding of the concept of nationalization shows that the purpose which the state first and foremost has as its aim in carrying out nationalization is an alteration in the economic distribution. No longer — in certain countries — shall a handful of the country's inhabitants possess capital goods and utilize them at the expence of other people, but the capital of industry, the mineral riches of the earth, etc. shall be nationalized and become the common property of the nation.

These political theories, according to which the removal of private ownership in favour of common national ownership is a goal in itself, have played an important part in the policy of nationalization in its earliest form as we know it from Soviet Russia. This ideological motive based on Marxist theories has nowadays — as will be shown later on — been pushed somewhat into the background(2), and the motive behind nationalization, in so far as it is directed against alien property must be sought moreover in the nationalism which has come to the fore since then.

The nationalistic trends which are to be seen very clearly in smaller states express themselves in the desire to carry on their own independent policy to the fullest possible extent without interference on the part of other states. The consequence of this view in the realm of economics, then, is that by nationalization the states seek to throw off the dependence that results from the foreign capital invested in their country.

That these views, the socialistic and the nationalistic, have been the decisive motive behind certain acts of nationalization in later

(1) Friedman, *op. cit.*, p. 14 ff., mentions in this connection, among several other examples, the dissolution of the feudal system after the French Revolution.

(2) Doman, *op. cit.*, p. 1125, states inter alia that the word socialization at any rate in legal linguistic usage has been displaced by nationalization, since this latter term draws attention to circumstances connected with national sovereignty rather than to socialism.

years appears clear, for example, from the following statement with which the Roumanian government accompanied the Nationalization Law of 11th June, 1948:

> "The nationalization of the principal enterprises consolidates our economic and political independence, fortifies the forces in their struggle against the attempt of interference with our internal matters and rape of our independence, carried on by the Anglo-American imperialists. It stresses our role as an active factor of the democratic and antiimperialistic front"(1).

Outside Soviet Russia and the countries of Eastern Europe these acts of nationalization dictated by nationalistic and socialistic motives have occurred e.g. in Mexico in 1938, in connection with the nationalization of the oil industry that was controlled by foreign interests; in Iran, where the Iranian oil industry was nationalized by an enactment of 2nd May, 1951, and in Egypt by the law of 26th July, 1956, where the Suez Maritime Canal Company was nationalized.

Considering the matter from this angle, that nationalization is dictated solely by the political motives referred to, we might expect to find that the nationalization of certain — and in some cases very extensive — parts of a country's industry was merely a single step in the removal of private ownership and the total exclusion of foreign investments.

This has, however, not been the case, apart from the acts of nationalization carried out in Soviet Russia immediately after the revolution.

After the conclusion of the Second World War no states, either in connection with nationalization or by any other means, have abolished private ownership. On the contrary several examples are to be found of a state, after the nationalization of the chief industries, banks, insurance companies, etc. having officially declared that it was not desired either now or in the future to increase the extent of nationalization. Declarations of this kind were(2) issued in Hungary in March 1948, and in Poland, where in connection with the nationalization laws a law was enacted "concerning the establishment of new undertakings and assistance to private initiative in industry and commerce". In pursuance of this law, any person — even foreigners — who wishes to start a new enterprise can obtain a written declaration to the effect that the enterprise will not be nationalized. According to Doman, this law was received with a certain amount of scepticism.

(1) Doman, *op. cit.*, p. 1128.

(2) According to Doman, *op. cit.*, p. 1126.

The fact that declarations concerning private investments were issued simultaneously with the nationalization laws, and thus could not have been motivated by the failure of the acts of nationalization to achieve their purpose, indicates that nationalization is also dictated by considerations of practical economy. Such considerations are in part of a general character, and partly the result of the special conditions which resulted from the Second World War.

Among these general considerations, first and foremost can be mentioned that of modern technical delevopment which has entailed the need for large scale activity. Machinery to replace manpower or increase its efficiency often demands co-operation between several undertakings if the exploitation of the equipment is to pay its way. It might be difficult to arrange co-operation of this nature between a large number of private managements. It might be countered — at any rate in communities based on the liberal economic view — that it ought to be in the private managements own interest to rationalize production, and that free competition would drive them to seek the most effective means of production.

In Great Britain it has, however, become apparent that such views do not apply, and that in so far as regards the production of goods essential to the community (public utilities, electricity, transport, etc.) or to the export trade (coal, iron and steel), it has been considered insufficient to leave the regulation of these means of production to private managements(1).

And so it is characteristic of British nationalization that in the period between the two world wars the government attempted to rationalize transport, electricity and the mining industry by the introduction of organs of control and appeals for co-operation in the introduction of new methods (particularly in the mining industry) and uniform tariffs. These appeals, however, achieved no results(2), and as the outcome of the desire to make British industries efficient for the purpose of the British export drive nationalization of these industries was carried out.

That ideological views to a certain extent had a part in the introduction of nationalization appears, however, from the fact that British politicians at public meetings held during the preparation of the Acts agitated for nationalization inter alia by describing the railways

(1) Cf. Heillroner, *Labor Unrest in the British Nationalized Sector*, Social Research, vol. 19, (1952), p. 61 ff.

(2) The British coal industry in 1938 produced 227 million tons of coal, whereas production in 1945 amounted to 174 million tons. This decline may be ascribed solely to inefficiency of production.

due for nationalization as "your railways"(1), and similary, on the 1st January, 1947 (the day the state took over) there appeared placards at the nationalized coal mines with the following inscription: "This colliery is now managed by the National Coal Board on behalf of the People". These social-political motives, however, compared with the economic considerations, played but a subordinate role even in the British Labour Party(2).

Similar technical considerations in connectiton with the desire to introduce a planned economy in certain limited fields motivated the acts of nationalization carried out in France after the end of the Second World War(3).

In addition to the circumstances mentioned above, other practical economic conditions can motivate the taking over by the state of private property. Thus nationalization may be found necessary in order to create peace on the labour market (this was, inter alia, the case in France), in order to establish control of a monopoly (also in France), or state intervention can be motivated by the desire to effect social reforms that cannot be carried out by any other means (for example, in Mexico and Hungary).

While the above-mentioned motives may be behind nationalization at any period, the acts of nationalization of recent years were also motivated by the special circumstances resulting from the Second World War(4).

As a result of war events and the German Nazi ideology, many undertakings, when their owners fled from German occupied territories, were without management or were taken over by others. At the end of the war it was impossible in many cases to re-establish the original ownership, since the new proprietors had probably in the meantime put money into the businesses and undertaken reconstruction, and the former owners were either dead or did not wish to return to the countries from which they had fled(5).

---

(1) Cf. Scammel, *Nationalization in Legal Perspective,* vol. 5, Current Legal Problems, (1952), p. 41.

(2) The attitude of this Party to nationalization found expression at the Party Congress of 30th September 1953 when the motion for the nationalization of agricultural land was rejected by a large majority, since it was not thought that such nationalization would be beneficial for the economic development.

(3) The French Minister for National Economy, René Pléven, said on 3rd August 1945, during the debate on the nationalization laws in the French National Assembly: "Nous moderniser en nationalisant ou mourir". Cf. La Pradelle, *op. cit.*, p. 45 ff.

(4) Cf. Friedman, *op. cit.*, p. 29 ff.

(5) Cf. Robinson, *Reparations and Restitution in International Law,* The Jewish Yearbook of International Law, (1948), p. 203.

Such "abandoned" property was to a great extent nationalized by those states in which the property was situated, inter alia for the reason that this procedure was the easiest and most expedient way of providing a solution to the problem(1).

A similar process was employed in the case of property which had been annexed by enemy action in the occupied territories.

In addition there was the fact that wartime destruction in those countries which had been the scene of military action had created an enormous need for capital investment in new machines, plant, etc. The need for capital was so great that it was not to be expected that private investments would be sufficient. In such cases nationalization, with the access to state investment and state control that it brings, seemed to be a practical and possible way to revive industries affected by the war. These views were thus the basis of the Austrian laws of 26th July, 1946, for the nationalization inter alia of the most important undertakings in the iron and steel industry. In connection with this, the Austrian state invested about 3550 million Austrian schillings in the nationalized industry.

The above mentioned motives invoked by the states as the basis for extensive nationalization(2) demonstrate that nationalization is motivated by interests that are of decisive importance for the states. Quite apart from those cases where nationalization is dictated by circumstances which arose as a result of events during the Second World War, the question of carrying out a programme of nationalization would in many instances be decisive for the economic and political existence of the state introducing them, and this may be assumed to be true both of states whose form of government is based on socialist ideologies and of states which to a greater or lesser extent otherwise acknowledge liberalism to be the most expedient economic basis. It is not to be wondered at, therefore, that these acts of nationalization have also affected alien property where this has been essential to the purpose which the state wished to achieve.

---

(1) Cf. in this connection Oatman, *The Nationalization Program in Czechoslovakia*, Dept. St. Bul., vol. 15, (1946), p. 1020.

(2) The nationalization laws of the various countries are discussed later in § 12.

§ 4.
WHAT INTERESTS PROVIDE THE MOTIVE FOR A PROTEST AGAINST NATIONALIZATION?

While we have seen that it is extensive and important economic interests which provide the motive for nationalization, it is also true that the protests and opposition to nationalization in other states are likewise dictated by economic and political interests of no mean force. Such interests may affect the economy of the state concerned directly and indirectly.

The introduction of measures of nationalization against alien property will mean — if no compensation is paid to the person affected by the nationalization — that the foreign nationals suffer a financial loss, and that their country will ultimately — in addition to the loss to the national income — lose a proportion of the economic power that goes with the foreign investments.

The economic and political interests that are at stake here for the foreign states are often of a very extensive importance.

In this connection it may be mentioned by way of example that property owned abroad by the United States and American nationals in 1947 amounted to about $ 45.500 million(1), while British investments outside the British Commonwealth in 1949 were in the region of £ 2000 million(2). As regards the individual states that carried out measures of nationalization it may be mentioned that in 1939 the foreign investments in Polish commercial and industrial companies amounted to $ 19.6 million, constituting 32.7 % of the total capital of Polish companies(3). In the years following the First World War Czechoslovakia carried out the nationalization of agricultural land, comprising 24 % of the total area of the state(4), but only 57½ % of the land affected which belonged to its own nationals, the rest being the property of foreigners(5) (6).

(1) Cf. Dickens and Will Harvey Reeves, *Foreign Investments*, Political Science Quarterly, (1949), p. 211.

(2) Cf. Schwarzenberger, *British Property Abroad*, Current Legal Problems, vol. 5, (1952), p. 296.

(3) According to *Yearbook of Poland*, (1939), quoted from Doman, *op. cit.*, p. 1146.

(4) Cf. Moodie, *Agrarian Reform in East Central Europe*, Yearbook of World Affairs, (1954), p. 242.

(5) Cf. Hobza, *Annuaire*, vol. 43, I, (1950), p. 85.

(6) The Treaties of Compensation shown in Part III, *infra*, give some indication of the size of the investments of the various countries in the nationalized states.

The interests of protecting property invested abroad also exist — though hardly to the same extent — in case of states which pay full compensation to aliens affected by the nationalization, since after all the effect of nationalization is to exclude foreign nationals from the activity within the economic sphere in which they had hitherto been engaged. This, too, would have an important effect on the economic power that goes with foreign investments.

The desire to oppose the direct and indirect effects of nationalization on capital invested abroad is also to be found even in states which have nationalization in their own country, cf. the stipulations included at the instigation of Sovjet Russia in the Bulgarian and Roumanian nationalization laws, in pursuance of which Sovjet Russian property was exempted from the nationalization measures, infra § 12.

In the case of states which do not themselves recognize nationalization as a means to the solution of economic problems, there will frequently be a further ground for protesting against nationalization in foreign countries which affects their interests.

A protest against nationalization in a foreign state will in practice be taken as an announcement that the nationalization of foreign property is looked on as something inadmissible and undesirable, and such an announcement — especially in times when nationalization is spreading further and further — can be one of the factors whereby the protesting state tries to preserve the confidence of other countries in its economic system and in its capital market, a confidence that may be essential if the country in question is to retain the ability to obtain foreign capital.

In addition to the economic and political views that can motivate opposition or protest in regard to nationalization in other states there is another consideration that must be mentioned that could be of importance in this context. It is a fact that a person will feel a stronger sense of injury if his property is taken away by a foreign government, whether he is living in that country or not, than if a corresponding loss was occasioned by this own government.

This is due, in the first place, to the fact that broadly speaking the measures taken by a person's own government are looked on as something unavoidable which affects every member of the community in the interests of the common good, but only rarely is a similar feeling of solidarity to be found where a foreign state is concerned.

In the second place there will exist between a state and its nationals in other countries a very strong feeling of unity, so that an offence against the property of a national abroad will be felt to be an offence committed by the foreign state against the honour of the home country. Dunn(1) describes this external solidarity as "... a manifestation of the group-consciousness that is represented in the concept of nationality, and is in some degree connected with the idea of relative prestige and importance of the group as compared with other competing goups".

These basically emotional views, even if they lack rational foundations, and even if their effects are not always visible, must, however, be included as a factor of importance when attempting to assess the weight that can be attached to the protests of states against the measures of nationalization undertaken by foreign states.

§ 5.
THE CHARACTER OF INTERNATIONAL LAW

For the decision and settlement of legal disputes that arise when conflicting interests collide, there exists the prevalent law in force. In this respect, however, there are important differences between the national and the international communities, the effect being that in the national and the international communities the character and function of law is also different.

A. *Differences between the national and the international communities.*

The disparity between the two different forms of community of importance in the considerations of the national and the international legal system may in practice be described as follows:

1. *The objective difference:* The individual members of the community of international law — in contrast to the subjects of the national community — are few in number and there are differences between them. This fact results inter alia in great difficulty when it comes to setting up general rules in the international community, since "many problems of international law require a detailed individual decision, with due consideration for the special conditions in each state, rather than abstract regulation"(2).

(1) *Protection of Nationals,* (1932).
(2) Ross, *op. cit.*, p. 58.

2. *The subjective difference:* This difference, which is almost of a psychological nature, is based on the fact that the subjects bound by international law are always collectives. The effect of this is that the conflicts that arise between the individual members of the community of international law can be more difficult of solution than conflicts between individual persons, for a collection of individuals are often more aggressive ("United we stand") or more implacable than the single individual.

3. *The historical difference:* National communities where it is regarded as illegal to take the law into one's own hand and where, in the case of a breach of the law, prosecution is made by public authorities, have all probably gone through a historical evolution from communities where legal disputes were decided by public authorities (for example, in moots), but the execution of the law was left to the injured party or his family, to the system we know to-day, where the administration of the law is the monopoly of the state authorities. In the international community the evolution has not reached this stage. A monopoly of power which takes care of the upholding of the law in the whole gambit of substance and procedure does not exist, since each member is an independent power unit. This can mean that in practice no rules of law can be upheld in the face of a recalcitrant state that has a certain power, and also that where it is carried out the maintenance of the law may be somewhat fortuitous; and the result is that it must be the main task of international law to prevent collision between the individual power units.

B. *Differences between the national and the international legal systems.*

These differences between the national and the international communities are also reflected in the individual rules of international law. Whereas the content of the law and the duty to observe the rules in the national community are, in relation to the person subject to the law, determined by the relationship of superior and subordinate that exists between him and the superior state authorities, the content and binding force of international law is essentially determined by the following factors:

1. *Power:* In many cases the rules of international law are determined by the actual position of power, which is invested with legal validity. This appears clearly when we think of the provisions laid down in peace treaties and the rules governing the territorial limitations of

states. The idea of the content of legal rules being determined by the actual position of power is to a certain extent known also in municipal law, for example, in prescription; but whereas the national legal community possesses a machinery of power whereby the exercise of power by the subjects of the law is placed under certain restrictions, such as the passing of a certain period of time, a certain good faith etc., no such restrictions exists on the international exercise of power, although attempts have been made — without succes — to do this by rules against illegal warfare(1), etc.

The result is that the rules of international law, based thus upon a position of power, are changeable and dependent upon the balance of power at any given time between the individual states.

2. *Reciprocity:* Legal rules based upon this point of view are dictated by the self-interest of the various states, in that in order to obtain for itself a favourable legal position a state is compelled to accord to other states a corresponding legal position. ("We do justice that justice may be done in return") (2).

To this group of legal rules there belongs a very considerable part of international law, for example, the rules governing the rights of aliens, the international rules of warfare, together with the special limitations that ought to apply within the territorial juristiction of the states.

The rules that are founded on the idea of reciprocity are also changeable, since it may be expected that a state will commit a breach of the international legal rule when it no longer has any interest in itself profiting by the legal position which the rule aims at assuring.

3. *Legal attitude:* Rules that are founded solely upon an international legal attitude will often be a taking over of the principles of the national law contained in all the legal systems of the states that set the tone. For it will frequently — though not always — be the case that the legal attitude that finds expression in the national law of the states will be invoked and recognized also in the mutual relations between states.

The content of such international legal rules will as a result change with any changes in the national legal attitude.

4. *Common interest of the states:* Lastly there may be mentioned the rules that aim at a legal status that can only be achieved by

---

(1) Cf. Briand—Kellogg Pact of 1928, the United Nations Charter, Art. 2, Section 4.

(2) Andrews in *Russian Socialist Federated Soviet Republic v. Cibrario*, Court of Appeals of New York, (1923), 235 N. Y. 255.

co-operation between the states. As examples of these we may point to the rules to combat infectious diseases, rules governing postal conveyance, and international traffic communications.

C. *The significance of these differences.*

It is essential for the interpretation and appreciation of the rules of international law in certain spheres to have a clear understanding of the facts and circumstances discussed above, which determine the character of the international legal system and the content of its rules; it will then be plain that the interest of the states in the international legal rules is a relative one. As the balance of power shifts, as the interests of the individual states change and/or old-established legal attitudes within the states are abandoned and replaced by new ones, this will bring about a change of content in the international legal rules.

There is incidentally nothing peculiar about this since the same holds good of municipal law. But in the national community the law is changed by superior organs of state, whereas the changes in international law are normally brought about by states committing a breach of the international legal rules (1). For it is characteristic of the breach of international law (except in the matter of an isolated case) that it is not necessarily — as in the case of a breach of the municipal law — an expression of the fact that the law-breaker recognizes the law per se, but desires a more favourable position for himself. A breach of international law must often be considered as a reaction against the existing content of the law which is now desired to change. The dispute concerning a breach of the existing law develops into a dispute concerning creating new law.

As a result we see that the rules of international law which regulate the international effects of nationalization must be understood (or laid down) on the basis of a close examination of the actual interests of the states rather than on the basis of a practice that has developed in quite different political and economic circumstances.

Only if this is observed the rules of international law will prove fit to solve the conflicts arising out of nationalization between such fundamental economic and political interests.

---

(1) Cf. Niemeyer, *Law without Force*, (1941), p. 9.

§ 6.
DELIMITATION OF THE PROBLEM

Since this study only deals with the international problems that have arisen as a result of nationalization, it is necessary to undertake a classification of the situations that arise or might be expected to arise when nationalization is carried out. These situations may contain problems of national law, international law or private international law, partly depending on the location of the nationalized property and partly determined by the character of the nationalized property — whether it is national or alien. Property is here designated as national when it belongs(1) to a physical or juridical person bound by bonds of nationality to the nationalizing state.

The following possible problems occur:

A. *The nationalized property is situated in the territory of the nationalizing state.*

1. The property is national.

   The legal problems arising here between the nationalizing state and its citizens, such as, for example, claims for compensation, fall outside the ambit of international law, since international law does not cover the legal relation between a state and its citizens. The problem is one of national law.

2. The property is alien.

   The legal problems arising here between the nationalizing state and foreign nationals (or their home country) are within the sphere of regulation by international law.

B. *The nationalized property is situated outside the territory of the nationalizing state.*

1. The property is national.

   (a) The legal problems arising here between the nationalizing state and the nationals affected by the nationalization fall outside the ambit of international law(2), cf. supra A 1.

---

(1) Concerning the legitimacy of this delimitation see *infra* § 17.

(2) Poul Andersen, *op. cit.*, p. 729, quotes as an example of public acquisition of citizens' property situated abroad, the Danish Supply of Goods Act. No. 406 of 3rd August 1940, § 5, in pursuance of which the Ministry of Trade could

(b) The relations between the nationalizing state and the state in which the property is situated can give rise to two different questions:

1°. The question whether the judicial authorities in the state where the property is situated are bound to co-operate in the execution of the nationalization. This problem is traditionally taken to be included in private international law, since in these cases it is a question of what national law is to apply.

2°. The question of the legal status of the nationalized property if the nationalization is recognized. This question — so far as regards the special rules governing the immunity of state property — is covered by the rules of international law.

2. The property is alien.
This situation might be imagined if the nationalization includes claims against nationals — either persons or companies — and the claims belong to foreign nationals living abroad, since according to the current legal view the nationality of a claim is determined by the nationality of the creditor. As a basis for the delimitation of this study the decisive fact must be that the question of the nationalization of the claims becomes of practical importance only at the moment when the creditor is enforcing his claim, and the place where this occurs thus must seem to be decisive for the territorial status of the claim, cf. a Danish judgment of 1952 (1), which deals with the claim of a nationalized Czech company against a Danish undertaking. Although the creditor was a Czech company, which at the time of nationalization was situated in Czechoslovakia, it was implied in the judgment that the claim »was situated« in Denmark, and that the rules of private international law governing the exclusive territorial validity of laws of expropriation and nationalization were decisive for the outcome of the case (2). In consequence a distinction may be made between the following situations:

---

take over also goods lying abroad "... if they belong to Danish nationals or undertakings."

(1) U. f. R., 1952, p. 856.

(2) Cf. also Seidl-Hohenveldern, *Internationales Konfiskations- und Enteignungsrecht,* (1952), p. 88 ff., p. 91.

(a) The claim is attempted to be enforced by execution against property situated abroad and belonging to a citizen in the nationalizing state. In that case the question of the legal effects of nationalization will be decided according to the rules of private international law, cf. supra. Here there are two possibilities:

1°. The nationalization is not recognized by the foreign state. In that case the claim can be executed, and no further problems arise.

2°. The nationalization is recognized by the foreign state. The creditor loses his claim and the question of the legality or otherwise of the nationalization etc. will be the province of international law.

(b) The claim is attempted to be enforced by execution against property situated in the nationalizing state. This situation is identical with that given under A 2. The case is thus covered by international law.

The cases that are relevant to international law are thus:

Case 1: A state nationalizes property that belongs to foreign states or alien physical and legal persons, and the property is situated either in the territory of the nationalizing state or outside it in a state which recognizes that nationalization has extraterritorial effects(1).

Case 2: A state nationalizes national property that is situated outside the territory of the nationalizing state in a state which recognizes that nationalization has extraterritorial effects.

The international legal problems that can arise in connection with Case 1 are, firstly, the question whether nationalization is *contrary to international law*, and this question will be dealt with infra in Part II; and secondly, the question whether nationalization also involves an *international duty for the nationalizing state to pay compensation.* This latter question will be dealt with infra in Part III.

In connection with Case 2 there arises the problem whether the property situated in a foreign country acquires, as a result of nationalization and of being taken over by the state, a special international status (immunity). This question will not come up for treatment in this study, since such a legal position — if it is recognized — must

(1) An examination of whether this is the case falls outside the province of the present study.

be understood as not being a specific effect of nationalization, since it does not follow from the rules applying to nationalization, but is the outcome of the application to the nationalized property of the ordinary rules of international law concerning state-owned property.

A more detailed definition of what is understood by property, what is decisive for a definition of the national character of property, and its territorial location, will be given later on in connection with a survey of the rules in resepect of which such closer definition is of importance.

As a starting point of this investigation it will suffice to designate the object affected by nationalization as "alien property".

PART II: LEGALITY

§ 7.
INTRODUCTION

In order to decide the question of whether the nationalization of foreign property can be regarded as legally justificable, it may seem natural to adopt the method employed in similar investigations concerning other forms of public interference with foreign property, for example, expropriation. The great majority of writers distinguish here between those forms of interference with foreign property which are accompanied by full compensation to the foreigner or to his home country and those where no compensation is paid. Whereas the former — in conformity incidentally with the constitutions of most civilized states — are regarded as lawful, the problems of international law — so these writers maintain — arises solely in the case of those where no compensation is accorded.

This traditional simplification of the nature of the problem, which appears to be influenced by the maxime of the protection of vested rights that is often referred to in the theory and practice of international law, seems here, however, to be inadequate.

This is due in the first place to the fact that the alien who, on an equal footing with nationals of the country concerned, receives full compensation when his property has to be surrendered to the state to be used for a purpose different from its previous one, can in all likelihood acquire with the compensation he received other property corresponding to the property expropriated, and so can continue his business in circumstances that do not necessarily vary much from those in which he was living and working before the expropriation; whereas the situation is completely different in the case of nationalization, even if compensation is paid. The typical case here is that the state appropriates for its own continued use an industrial activity together with its good-will with a view to continuing the business hitherto conducted by the nationalized activity. The owner of the property or activity — for the simple reason that his custom and his market are now reserved solely for the state — will not be in a position, no matter how large a sum he receives by way of compensation, to make any use of his experience in that particular sphere of business. The position of the former owner, whether it is a matter of a private person or a company, can thus be completely changed.

This difference in the situation of the foreign owner — even if full compensation is paid — in the case of nationalization compared with the case of expropriation will undoubtedly influence the attitude of the implicated states to the legality of the interference with the foreign property, to such an extent that it is reasonable to suppose that the rules of international law concerning the legality of a nationalization will not be determined, at any rate will not be determined exclusively, by the consideration whether the nationalization is accompanied by full compensation to those directely or indirectly affected by it or not.

In cases where not even nationalization accompanied by full compensation is in conformity with international law, it is obvious that nationalization without compensation to the victims of the same is not legally justificable. In addition, however, an independent investigation should be made to determine whether nationalization of foreign property otherwise, i.e. apart from the cases mentioned can be regarded as legally justified by a reference to international law even if compensation is not paid. If such nationalization may be regarded as justificable, those affected by the nationalization, or their home countries, cannot oppose the nationalization, nor claim recovery, i.e. the return of the property to the former owners(1).

It must be expressly stated that the inquiry into the latter problem, even if it should lead to the conclusion that nationalization of foreign property without payment of compensation is a legitimate step justified by international law, in no way renders superfluous the inquiry undertaken below in Part III into the question whether nationalization has the international effect that those affected by the same acquire an independent claim to compensation. For it is a phenomenon known also to the system of municipal law that certain acts (for example, the right of self-preservation in an emergency), considered desirable by the community, entail a duty to pay compensation to such persons as may suffer a loss through the said action. If such compensation it not paid, the act may still be considered lawful, but the omission to pay compensation is then an independent breach

---

(1) The question of the lawfulness of nationalization without payment of compensation incidentally is also of importance in private international law, viz., in determining whether the municipal court of a country according to the doctrine of ordre-public is bound to recognize the effects of such foreign nationalization within its jurisdiction.

of the law. Understood in this way, the liability to pay compensation is not a precondition for the lawfulness of the said act, but a result of the same.

§ 8.
SOURCES

International law is the body of rules governing the mutual relations of states, and international customary law so will find expression in all cases where the behaviour of the states indicates that such behaviour can be considered the result of a rule of international law. Such expression of international law can be objectivated particularly clearly in international judicial decisions. But treaties too, whether they are bilateral or collective, *can* provide evidence of a general conception of international customary law. It is not unusual in legal litteratur to find writers who deny the existence of international customary law when a treaty has been concluded on the question. For their view is that a treaty would be superfluous were its contents already valid international law. Such a reasoning is, however, not cogently necessary, and in many cases would be right-out wrong. A treaty is often concluded because from a technical and political point of view it is the easiest way to settle a minor legal dispute between the parties to the treaty in conformity with generally recognized international law, and frequently a treaty is the sole means of making a state alter municipal legislation that is in conflict with the customary rules of international law.

In addition, and this will be of special importance for this investigation, even if it cannot be substantiated that a bilateral treaty, for example, is the expression of an already existing conception of international law, the very fact that treaties of similar contents are frequently concluded concerning identical subjects can create a general legal attitude, thereby resulting in the creation of a definite conception of international customary law(1).

Besides an analysis of international practice and treaties it may be of importance to investigate the principle of muncipal law in individual states. As mentioned earlier on, a number of the rules af inter-

(1) Cf. the corresponding situation in municipal law, where the legal position of the citizens, whether expressed by statute or judicial practice, often is a codification of already existing customs concerning contracts, customs which have proved to be expedience in the behaviour of the citizens one to another.

national law must be regarded as an expression of the legal view of civilized states as manifested in their municipal law(1). If, for example, it is in accordance with the Danish and Swedish national legal conception that, for instance, *culpa* is an essential basis for the liability to pay compensation, it can hardly be expected that this view would be departed from in an international conflict between the two states. Nevertheless, a certain care must be exercised in drawing conclusions from even an unequivocal municipal conception of law in favour of a corresponding international one, since special circumstances have to be taken into account on the grounds that the subjects of international law are collective bodies, and collective interests in international relations may differ considerably from the interests of the state when regulating the behaviour of individuals in the national community(2), and also by reason of the special problems of evidence in international law, and the conditions for upholding the law, etc.

Subject to this latter reservation, municipal legislation and municipal judicial practice will also be included in this investigation.

§ 9.
STARTING POINT: THE PRINCIPLE OF TERRITORIAL JURISDICTION

The starting point for the rights and duties of states in the family of nations must be found in the fundamental rule of distribution of competence, the principle of territorial jurisdiction, according to which a state is competent, and solely competent, to do within its

---

(1) Friedman thinks otherwise, *op. cit.*, p. 111—115, and denies that the municipal law can provide any guide with regard to the rules of international law, since (i) the municipal law cannot be the expression of a *consensus gentium*, and (ii) if the rules of international law were dependent upon the municipal law the states could unilaterally alter the international law. Neither of these views however seems convincing, and in particular it should be observed that the fact that municipal law can be altered unilaterally and thereby influence the rules of international law is a point that is in agreement with the aspect of international law under consideration here in its character of a body of legal standards.

(2) Cf. *Giesler gegen Giesler Erben*, (1935), Schweiz Bundesgericht, Amtlische Sammlung 61, I, 258.

territory those acts which actually or potentially are done in the exercise of the governmental power of the state(1).

This rule gives to the state authority to act within its territory as it pleases free of any intervention on the part of other states. Its fundamental character and central position in the settlement of international disputes are deeply rooted in the aims and purposes of international law. The system of international law, unlike the municipal systems, exactly is not the expression of a social policy as its contents, to the effect that certain political interests such as, for example, full employment, or liberal economy, have priority to others. The sole policy of international law is to avoid conflicts(2). In addition to this international law gives to the states within their territory a comprehensive freedom of action, the only limitation being that this freedom must not be exercised to prejudice the corresponding freedom of other states, or to prejudice the international intercourse in which all states have an interest in — though such interest may be of varying nature.

This view of international law becomes particularly clear when considering the law of aliens, i.e. the rules which bind the state to a given behaviour towards aliens or alien property in its territory.

In accordance with the principle of territorial jurisdiction the alien — and the alien property — is subject to the territorial competence of the state where he lives, as the case may be where the property is situated. This rule, however, without any limitations, would deprive the alien of any international protection, but as a matter of fact it is subject to substantial modifications dictated by the common interest in international intercourse, and the question consequently is whether such modifications exist with regard to the nationalization of alien property, and if so, how they can be enforced.

---

(1) Cf. Ross, *op. cit.*, p. 138, and Hans Kelsen, *Principles of International Law*, (1952), p. 242.

(2) However, an attempt has been made by the adoption by the United Nations of the Universal Declaration of Human Rights to give to international law an aspect of social policy.

§ 10.
SPECIAL RULES REGARDING STATE PROPERTY

By way of introduction an attempt will be made to ascertain whether the special rules of international law regarding state property are of importance in deciding the attitude to nationalization of such property.

It is generally assumed that the states and their property in foreign countries are immune in the sense that execution against such property or other economic interference with such property cannot take place by the action of the state, where it is situated. Attempts have been made to base this principle of the immunity of state property, which is a limitation to the territorial jurisdiction of the state where the property is situated, on the general principle of equality, the doctrine of sovereignty, the independence of the states, or on mere practical principles of reciprocity(1).

In this connection, however, there arises the question whether international legal immunity can be upheld in so far as regards state-owned industrial undertakings. This problem came up for a legal decision in the case of *Ulen & Co. v. Bank Gospodarstwa Krajowego* (1940).(2) The defendants were a Polish bank, which in its by-laws was described as a "state institution with independent legal capacity", 60 % of the bank's capital belonged to the Finance Department and other institutions; the bank was under the control of the Finance Minister, and the net profit was to go to the Polish Finance Department. It was held in the judgment that this Polish bank had no part in the immunity accorded to state property. The case thus clearly demonstrates that immunity at any rate does not extend to state activities which are to be regarded as independent units.

In cases where the property is directly state-owned and exploited by the state for commercial or industrial purposes it must, however, be accepted that the rules concerning state immunity have no significance either for state property used in this way. This is on account of the contents of the rule of immunity as accepted by the most modern practice of states. Such commercial or industrial state property may be an industrial activity situated in a foreign country and acquired by the state under a peace treaty, or may be property in a foreign country where a branch of a state activity is located, or may be shares

(1) Cf. the decision quoted below the *Case of the Cristina*, (1938).
(2) The United States, Supreme Court of New York, 24. N. Y. S. (2d) 201.

in foreign activities or in commercial state-owned ships calling at foreign ports.

In England this problem was adjudicated upon in the *Case of the Cristina* (1938).(1) The case referred to a merchant ship that had been requisitioned by the Spanish Republican Government, on whose behalf it was seized by the Spanish consul. The ship was to be used as an official state ship and its immunity was recognized. In the opinion of some of the judges, however, it was indicated that the result would have been different if the ship had been requisitioned by the state to be run as a commercial vessel. On this point it is stated:

> "When the doctrine of the immunity of the person and property of foreign sovereigns from the jurisdiction of the courts of this country was first formulated and accepted it was a concession to the dignity, equality and independence of foreign sovereigns which the comity of nations enjoined. It is only in modern times that sovereign states have so far condescended to lay aside their dignity as to enter the competitive markets of commerce, and it is easy to see that different views may be taken as to whether an immunity conceded in one set of circumstances should to the same extent be enjoyed in totally different circumstances ...".

In French practice(2) it is now accepted that execution may be levied against commercial property of foreign states cf. in this connection *State v. Vestvig et al* (1944),(3) where it was held that execution could take place against property belonging to the Free Norwegian government.

The newest American practice also accepts the view that international legal immunity does not apply in cases where the state is acting *jure gestionis*.

The development in the rules of international law that has been demonstrated in the judicial practice quoted above and which means that states when carrying on industrial or commercial activities cannot claim special privileges for the property invested in such activities — also from a practical view — seems reasonable. When the state acts as shipowner, exporter and importer, owner of purely commercial or industrial activities and thus puts itself on an equal footing with private citizens, the state must also bear the risk associated therewith.

Concerning the problem of the illegality of nationalization, it must follow from what has been set forth here that the nationalization of

(1) House of Lords, [1938], A. C. 485.

(2) Castel, "Immunity of a Foreign State from Execution, French Practice", *A. J. I. L.*, vol. 46, (1952), p. 520—526.

(3) Cours de Cassation, *Annual Digest of International Law*, (1946), no. 32.

alien property serving an official state purpose, must be considered as being in conflict with international law even if full compensation is paid by the nationalizing state. As far as state property serving commercial interests is concerned, nationalization of such property must be judged according to the rules governing foreign property in general. The special rules of state immunity do not extend to such cases.

§ 11.

IS THE EQUALITY OF ALIENS WITH THE COUNTRY'S OWN NATIONALS ESSENTIAL FOR THE FULFILMENT OF THE REQUIREMENTS OF INTERNATIONAL LAW?

(THE THEORY OF NON-DISCRIMINATION)

It is generally recognized that aliens have no claim to equality with the nationals of the country in so far as *rights* are concerned(1). Thus, in nearly every state, there is discrimination between aliens and nationals as regards political rights, the exercise of which can influence the form of government of the country, just as the rights of aliens are often limited in respect of employment, the holding of real property, or the exercise of trade and business, etc. The limitations which international law contain concerning the power of states to exercise such discrimination are to be found in special treaties and can hardly be taken as having the validity of generally recognized international law.

On the other hand states are bound to give to the foreigner the same *protection* as is accorded to the country's own nationals in respect of his person and property(2). A lower degree of protection for the foreigner in this respect will be taken as a breach of the international law of aliens and will incur liability for the state of residence(3). This must be taken to apply even where the protection

(1) Cf. Oppenheim—Lauterpacht, *International Law*, (1947), vol. I, p. 628 ff.

(2) *Ibid.*, p. 627: "Every state is by the Law of Nations compelled to grant to aliens at least equality before the law with its citizens, as far as safety of person an property is concerned".

(3) Cf. inter alia the case of the *Norwegian Shipowner's Claim against the United States*, (1922), *Report of International Arbitration Awards*, vol. I, p. 307.

accorded to the foreigner exceeds in effectiveness and extent the customary protection accorded in the foreigner's home country, since the mere discrimination in the wrong direction would be taken by the foreigner's home country as an affront to their honour.

It must therefore follow that nationalization directed against both nationals and foreigners must be illegal if in similar situations the interests of foreigners are given a lower degree of protection than those of the nationals of the country concerned, cf. for example the Polish Nationalization Law of 3rd January, 1946, Art. 6, in pursuance of which Polish public juridical persons obtained a preferential position in respect of claims against nationalized activities as compared with foreign private persons or companies who held similar claims.

It is possible, however, to raise the question as to whether nationalization measures, be it in the form of a statute law or an administrative act, directed against a whole branch of industry or against all activities of a certain size, must be regarded as contrary to international law in those cases where all the undertakings affected by the nationalization are the property of foreigners. An example of this kind is afforded by the Mexican nationalization of the oil industry in 1938, which industry was based entirely on foreign capital(1), and also by the Iranian nationalization in 1951 of the oil industry. In spite of the general terms of the Iranian Law, it applied only to property belonging to the British company, The Anglo-Iranian Oil Company, which held the monopoly of oil production(2). A most recent case is afforded by the Egyptian Nationalization Law of 26th July, 1956, directed solely against the Suez Maritime Canal Company which is based on foreign capital(3).

If raised, however, this question must be answered in the negative, as the rules of international law against discrimination can be considered to be satisfied when foreigners are given formal equality with the nationals of the country in question in respect of protection in similar situations.

If therefore according to the municipal law property is not protected against acts of nationalization, and a state carries out such an act, by general criteria it will not be possible on the basis of the formal demand for equality to make out a case of liability against the

(1) Cf. Gaither, *Expropriation in Mexico*, (1940), p. 9.
(2) Cf. infra § 12.
(3) Cf. *White Paper on the Nationalization of the Suez Maritime Canal Company*, Published by the Government of Egypt on the 12th of August 1956.

nationalizing state, even though in actual fact the nationalization measures affect foreigners only. There is no unlawful discrimination here(1)(2).

§ 12.

IS THE EQUALITY OF ALIENS WITH THE COUNTRY'S OWN NATIONALS SUFFICIENT FOR THE FULFILMENT OF THE REQUIREMENTS OF INTERNATIONAL LAW?

Whereas the equality of foreigners with the country's own nationals — in so far as regards the protection of property against nationalization — is essential for the fulfilment by a state of its international obligations in respect of the international law of aliens, there is no agreement as to whether such equality is also sufficient.

Thus, some writers hold that the alien has not in his capacity of a non-national of the state any special claim for protection of his property. When an alien takes up residence in a country, or invests his capital there, he must share the conditions of that country's own nationals. The fact that aliens acquire property does not impose a restriction on the sovereign legislature and its power to give rules respecting property situated in its territory on such lines as will best serve the interests of the community(3).

Other writers take the opposite view, viz., that the status of an alien is independent of the fact that the country's own nationals may be given an identical treatment(4).

---

(1) Cf. Danish Law No. 132 of 30th March, 1946, concerning the confiscation of German and Japanese property, which deprived German and Japanese nationals of the general protection accorded in Denmark to private property. This was a case of illegal discrimination, from the point of international law, which could only be justified by the special circumstances which gave rise to the particular law.

(2) A different view is expressed by Friedman, *op. cit.*, p. 212, who holds in case of expropriation that in such a situation there is no longer equality between the foreigners affected and the nationals not affected when it is a question of their share in the national financial burdens.

(3) Cf. Fischer—Williams, *op. cit.*, p. 1 ff., also Strupp, *Das völkerrechtliche Delikt*, (1920), p. 118, and also the references given in Bindschedler, *Verstaatlichungsmassnahmen und Entschädigungspflicht nach Völkerrecht*, (1950), p. 10 ff.

(4) Cf. Fachiri, "Expropriation and International Law", *British Yearbook of International Law*, vol. 6, (1925), p. 159 ff., and La Pradelle, *op. cit.*, p. 59.

The problem of the relationship between the legal status of nationals and aliens has been clearly formulated in practice, inter alia by the United States Government in a Note of 28th August, 1953, to the Government of Guatemala, on the occassion of the encroachment by the latter Government on land belonging to an American corporation, United Fruit Company. The American Note states:

> "... Further the United States Government must point out that international law does not authorize states to do any and every act, so long as such act is imposed on nationals and foreigners on a basis of equality or with-out discrimination. What a state may do with respect to its nationals or their property is a matter largely between that state and its nationals, for the reason that nationals of a state are presumed to be able to take corrective measures looking to the protection of their rights.
>
> The Government of the United States is warranted in expecting not only that the law of Guatemala shall be applied fairly as to American nationals without discrimination, but also that both the law itself and its application shall conform at least to minimum standards required by international law".(1)

This note inter alia bears out one point, namely, that the question raised here is closely connected with — or rather, is another aspect of — the question whether in the international law of aliens there exists a minimum standard that must be observed if nationalization it to be lawful. Only in case this question is answered in the affirmative equality between nationals and aliens will not *per se* be sufficient to meet the requirements of international law, viz., if in such a situation a treatment that does not come up to the minimum standard required is accorded to the alien.

The rules of international law in this respect may be found both in special treaties and in generally accepted international law.

A. *Treaty provisions concerning the protection of alien property.*

In cases where a treaty contains regulations prohibiting a state from acts of dispossession of property belonging to one of the contracting parties or its nationals, and where the provisions of the treaty are taken to apply also to nationalization, it must be taken for granted that the nationalization of such property must be contrary to international law. This follows from the principle of the binding force of agreements, *pacta sunt servanda,* long established in international law, and in this connection, therefore it makes no

(1) Cf. *Dep. St. Bul.*, vol. 29, (1953), p. 358.

difference if the nationalization is also directed against the country's nationals.

To further the development of international relations there have been concluded in the course of the last 100 years a number of treaties containing provisions concerning the protecting of property. As instances of this widespread treaty-practice there may be mentioned the treaties of domicilation between Switzerland and the United States of 5th November, 1850, between Switzerland and Roumania of 19th Juli, 1933(1), the treaty of 15th Juli, 1931, between the United States and Poland concerning friendship, trade and consular rights(2), a similar treaty between the United States and Hungary dated 1926(3), and various commercial treaties concluded by the Soviet Union with a number of countries, for example, with Italy, 7th March, 1924, Germany, 12th October, 1925(4), and Denmark, 17th August, 1946(5). A more recent example is afforded by the treaty between the United States and Italy of 2nd February, 1948, a treaty of friendship, commerce and maritime affairs(6).

It is typical of all these treaty provisions, however, that where they deal with property other than state property they in no case preclude acquisition of property by the state in the interests of the common good. It is, on the contrary, implied, that such acts can take place. The treaty referred to above between the United States and Italy of 2nd February, 1948, includes the following provisions in Art. 5, Section 2:

> "The property of nationals corporations and associations of either High Contracting Party shall not be taken within the territories of the other High Contracting Party without due process of law and without the prompt payment of just and effective compensation . . .".

Such a provision in a treaty cannot be taken as a prohibition of nationalization, but can at the most(7) mean that a certain procedure shall be observed, and that compensation shall be paid, and it is

(1) Cf. Bindschedler, *op. cit.*, p. 11.

(2) Cf. *Dep. St. Bul.*, vol. 24, (1951), p. 821.

(3) *Ibid.*, vol. 22, (1950), p. 399.

(4) Bindschedler, *loc. cit.*

(5) The treaty which supersedes the earlier treaty of 23rd April, 1923, contains only the most favoured nations clause in Art. 13, for this see infra.

(6) Briggs, *The Law of Nations*, (1953), p. 542.

(7) Section 3 of the same provision includes the most favoured nation clause usual in such treaties, according to which aliens shall not receive treatment that is inferior to that accorded to the nationals of the country of residence, nor to that accorded to the nationals of the third state, which at the time is

therefore unnecessary with regard to the question of the possible illegality of acts of nationalization to make any further attempt to ascertain whether or not the treaties can cover such acts of dispossession.

On the other hand, the most favoured nation clauses contained in such treaties in connection with other circumstances may lead to the result that the nationalization of alien property must unconditionally be regarded as being contrary to international law.

This was indeed the case, for example, with regard to the acts of nationalization that took place in Roumania. By the peace treaty of 10th February, 1947, Art. 31 c(1), Roumania entered into the following obligation:

> "United Nations nationals, including juridical persons, shall be granted national and most-favoured nation treatment in all matters pertaining to commerce, industry, shipping and other forms of business activity within Roumania . . .".

The Roumanian Nationalization Law of 11th June, 1948, however, made an exception of property belonging to Soviet Russia(2). This led to Notes from the United States, dated 7th September, 1948(3) and 7th March, 1949(4), protesting to the Roumanian government against the nationalization of American property, which was considered a breach of the provisions concerning equality contained in the treaty of peace. Accordingly, the United States asked that the principal property should be returned to its owners(5).

It is only on rare occasions, however, that we find instances of nationalization of foreign property that can be considered contrary to existing international law on the ground of its being incompatible with the provisions of special treaties. A few treaties nevertheless have given rise to legal proceedings, cf. for example, the *Case concerning certain German interests in Polish Upper Silesia* (1926)(6).

---

or in the future will be the most favoured. Whether, when this clause is considered, there is basis in the treaty for claims for compensation in cases where neither the nationals or the nationals of the third state are awarded compensation is not quite clear, though on a literal interpretation of the wording this seems to be precluded.

(1) *U. N. Treaty Series*, vol. 42, (1949), p. 66.

(2) The same was incidentally the case in Bulgaria.

(3) *Dep. St. Bul.*, vol. 19, (1948), p. 408.

(4) *Dep. St. Bul.*, vol. 20, (1949), p. 391.

(5) *Ibid.*, p. 392.

(6) *P. C. I. J. Series A*, No. 7.

B. *The maxim of vested rights.*

1. *The traditional view.* The maxim of the protection of the so called vested rights (*droits aquis, wohlerworbene rechte, jura quasita*) has its foundation in municipal law, more precisely, intertemporal law and international private law(1).

In *intertemporal law* it is accepted that, in the application of a new law the judge must imply that it was not the purpose of the new law to violate vested rights which have come into existence and have been recognized by earlier legislation. The principle of respect for vested rights has, however no binding force on the legislator, for a law is not invalid solely because it may intend to violate vested rights. Understood in this manner the theory of protection of vested rights is merely another aspect of the generally recognized principle that laws should not have a retroactive effect.

The maxim of vested rights is also accepted to play — although this is disputed — a role in *private international law* when the question is to be decided whether a right that has been acquired under the legal system of a foreign civilized country must be recognized by the courts(2).

From these two original spheres of application in municipal law the concept of vested rights has found its way into international law, where the theory as to the protection of these rights is to the effect that the power, which, by virtue of the principle of territorial jurisdiction, the country of residence has over persons and property in its territory, is modified in favour of the vested rights of alien citizens, corporations and associations.

The doctrine finds widespread — although qualified — support in international legal opinion, where some writers plead it in support of the rules of international law concerning nationalization. The maxim of respect for vested rights is then regarded as part of the international legal standard to be observed unconditionaly by a state in its behaviour towards aliens.

The treaties of domiciliation and friendship mentioned above in Section A, according to which private property is apparently assured a specially favourable position, are often quoted in support of the maxim. The line of thought in this case is that these treaties are regarded as the product of a generally recognized rule of internatio-

---

(1) Cf. Kaeckenbeeck, "The protection of Vested Rights", *British Yearbook of International Law*, vol. 17, (1936), p. 2 ff.

(2) *Ibid.*, p. 6, and Friedman, *op. cit.*, p. 121.

nal law concerning the protection of vested rights, so that such a rule must also hold good in cases where no treaty has been concluded between the parties involved. Finally, the maxim is considered to be borne out by international judical practice and by international arbitration as well as by a number of diplomatic decisions respecting the protection of property.

2. *Critical valuation.* The body of international decisions which are pleaded in support of the maxim under discussion and the categorical support given to the same by a number of writers of high repute, cf. among others, Anzilotti(1), Verdross(2), Anderson(3), Scelle(4), Doman(5), Hyde(6), Woolsey(7) and Bindschedler(8), would appear, however, to be of little weight in the determination of the legality of nationalization. The explanation of this obviously is that the decisions in question were made in — and belong to — a period when liberal economy was the only recognized economic system in the leading states. Respect for vested rights in municipal law, and the uniformity of the economic systems of the leading countries in so far as their views of private property were concerned, simply was the pre-condition for the assumption of the existence in international law of a maxim of protection for vested rights(9). Further, the number of cases where a state wanted to aquire foreign-owned private property under compulsory powers were extraordinarily few and — for the aquiring state — of minor importance(10).

(1) *Cours de droit international,* vol. I, p. 473.
(2) *Völkerrecht*, p. 220.
(3) "Title to Confiscated Property", *A. J. I. L.*, vol. 20, (1926), p. 528.
(4) *Précis de Droit de Gens,* vol. II, p. 113 ff.
(5) *Op. cit.*, p. 1127 ff.
(6) *International Law,* vol. I, (1947), p. 713 ff.
(7) "Expropriation of Oil Properties in Mexico", *A. J. I. L.*, vol. 32, (1938), p. 519.
(8) *Op. cit.*, p. 8 ff.
(9) Cf. Lord Palmerston's instruction to the British diplomatic representative in Athene in the *Finlay Case* (1849): "In all countries it is understood that when land belonging to a private individual is required for purposes of great public utility or of national defence, the private rights must so far yield to public interest, that the individual is compelled by law to give up his land to the public, provided always that he shall receive for it from the public its full and fair value ...", and the British Note in the *Expropriated Religious Properties Case* (1920): "Respect for property, respect for acquired rights, these are principles of law in all civilized lands".
(10) Schwarzenberger, *British Property* ..., p. 299, says that the fact that the compensation money could freely be exchanged into foreign currency was likewise of importance for the working of the maxim of vested rights in international law.

The fact that the decisive economic basis of the maxim of the protection of vested rights has fundamentally changed also appears from the replies given by various countries as early as 1929 to The Preparatory Committee of the League of Nations for the Codification of International Law on the Responsibility of States for Damage caused in their Territory to the Person or Property of Foreigners(1), where it could be clearly seen that the maxim was not unanimously recognized.

Accordingly it must be reasonable to asume that the maxim of the protection of vested rights — already as a consequence of the change in the conditions and circumstances underlying the existence of the maxim — is of no importance in deciding what minimum standard in international law is to be observed unconditionally by states in their dealings with foreigners. With regard to the question under discussion, namely, whether nationalization without compensation can be regarded as legitimate by reference to the territorial jurisdiction of a state, the maxim of protection of vested right, at any rate, will give no assistance, as the maxim and the decisions referred to above provide no contribution to determine if payment of compensation is a pre-condition for the legality of the interference with private-owned foreign property in question, or if liability to pay compensation is the result of an interference with private-owned foreign property that is legal to all interests and purposes, but which, as mentioned, gives rise to a claim for compensation.

C. *The theory of the international minimum standard set by civilized states.*

The international legal minium standard for the behaviour of states towards foreigners is determined to a large extent by the fact that the foreigner has a claim to a legal treatment that is not less than that promised by the minimum claims of civilization(2). The determination of the content of this standard, however, can involve numerous and great difficulties.

1. *International resolutions, decisions, and treaties.* The problem of a common legal attitude as regards the demands of civilized states

(1) L. of N. Doc. C75, M69, 1929 V.

(2) Cf. in this connection *The Neer Claim,* (1926), United States-Mexico, General Claims Commission, *Opinion of Commissioners,* 1927, p. 71.

concerning the protection of property has been studied in recent years both by the League of Nations and the United Nations.

The protocol of the Convention which formed the basis for discussion at the Conference, summoned in 1929 by the League of Nations — referred to above — to consider the rights of aliens, contained in art. 11, section 5, views which support the opinion that there is no common international legal attitude to the problem under review. The Convention protocol gave rise to much discussion and was not adopted, and this may be taken as a sign of the confusion displayed at the Conference on this question.

Nor does the Universal Declaration of Human Rights adopted by the United Nations on 10th December, 1948, contain anything that can be taken to be an expression of an international legal attitude concerning protection as against acts of nationalization, since art. 17, section 2, providing that no one can be arbitrarily deprived of his property, is of no importance in this respect.

The matter of nationalization was discussed, however, in December 1952, in the Second Committee of the General Assembly of the United Nations, in connection with the deliberations on the right of the underdeveloped countries to exploit their natural wealth and resources(1). The Committee discussed a resolution proposed by Uruguay containing an appeal to the member states to respect the right of any state to nationalize its natural resources.

In the Committee there was general agreement that the right of a state to nationalize these interests was an inalienable sovereign right, recognized by the law of nations. Some states (Canada, China, Haiti, Honduras and Saudi Arabia), however, were of the opinion that it was unnecessary to adopt a resolution on the matter, whereas others (Australia, Belgium, Canada, Denmark, Great Britain, Holland, New Zealand, the Philippines, and others) held the view that the resolution ought to contain provisions concerning the liability to pay compensation in a case of nationalization of foreign interests. It was urged in the end (by Haiti, Great Britain, Sweden, and the Union of South Africa) that the question of nationalization was essentially within the domestic jurisdiction of any state, and therefore could not be regulated by the United Nations. After vain attempts — on the part of Holland — to get the matter referred to the judical committee, and — on the part of Denmark — to have the discussion of the question adjourned, and after the rejection of

---

(1) Cf. *Year Book of the United Nations*, (1952), p. 387—390, and *Dep. St. Bul.*, vol. 22, (1952), p. 399.

an American amendment, containing a provision that foreign interests in any case ought to be respected, the matter was sent to the General Assembly. On 21st December, 1952, the General Assembly adopted the resolution concerning the exploitation of natural resources, by 36 votes to 4, among them the United States and Great Britain, while 20 states abstained from voting (including France, Norway, Sweden and Denmark). In its final form the resolution contained an appeal to the member states "to refrain from acts, direct or indirect, designed to impede the exercise of the sovereignty of any state over its natural resources".

In view of the fact that the resolution dealt exclusively with natural resources in underdeveloped countries, and that the word "nationalization" as well as any reference to "international law" were deliberately omitted(1), the adoption of this resolution can hardly be considered as an indication of the existence of a common legal attitude to nationalization in general among the states which voted in favour of the adoption.

2. *The municipal laws of various nations.* In order to decide whether there exists in international law a generally accepted minimum standard prohibiting the nationalization of alien property without payment of compensation, it will thus be necessary to look af the national practice in the field of nationalization, and thereby try to ascertain wheteher nationalization without compensation is regarded by the states as a generally accepted form of interference with private property, or whether on the contrary nationalization without compensation must be regarded as an act which — considered from the standpoint of the majority of states — is unusual and in conflict with the view held by civilized states of the rights of the individual. In the latter case nationalization of foreign property without compensation must be held to be undesirable in the international community, and such nationalization would then be against the international legal minimum standard to be unconditionally upheld in so far as concerns the property of aliens.

The following details will throw light on the attitude of the states to nationalization:

a. *Austria.* Among other reasons, in order to assist industry hit by the war, Austria passed the nationalization laws of 26th July, 1946(2) and

(1) Cf. the statement by India in the General Assembly, in connection with the proposal of an amendment, *Year Book of the United Nations,* (1952), p. 389. Cf. also Cheng, "International Law in the United Nations", *Year Book of World Affairs,* (1954), p. 174—175.

(2) Bundesblatt für 16/9 1946.

26th March, 1947. In pursuance of these laws nationalization was effected of the large credit institutions, the most important coal mines, the most important undertakings in the iron and steel industry, and the most important activities engaged in the extraction of crude oil, together with a number of engineering work, traffic activities and electricity undertakings.

In all the laws affected 70 concerns, employing about 98,000 persons, or 22 % of those employed in Austrian industries. In connection with this nationalization the Austrian state undertook extensive investment in the activities (1).

The nationalization laws provided that compensation should be paid in accordance with stipulations to be laid down by law.

b. *Bulgaria.* As long ago as the Law of 25th December, 1942, the Bulgarian banks became nationalized (2). The Law provided that compensation should be paid to the holders of bank shares in proportion to the face value of the shares. Compensation for shares belonging to foreigners was however to be arranged after further negotiation with the governments involved.

With authority derived from the Bulgarian Constitution of 4th December, 1947, there was enacted, with effect from 23rd December, 1947, a general nationalization law, whereby large parts of industry were transferred to state ownership.

With special reference to foreign property this Law in Art. 4 declares that the nationalization does not cover undertakings belonging to foreign nations *and* covered by the provision in Art. 24 of the Peace Treaty of 10th February, 1947. Since this latter provision, however, exclusively deals with the recognition by Bulgaria of the right of Soviet Russia to German property in Bulgaria (3), the effects of Art. 4 of the Law are restricted to Russian property.

Art. 13 of the Law contains provisions concerning the duty of the state to pay compensation to former owners. According to Art. 14 collaborators and persons otherwise under political disability are not entitled to receive compensation.

c. *Burma.* In 1948 an extensive land reform was carried out, which was regarded as the first step towards the collectivization of agriculture. Forestry, river transport and the oil industry were subsequently nationalized, in such a way, however, that the former owners of the nationalized undertakings received compensation (4).

---

(1) For this see supra § 3.
(2) Doman, *op. cit.*, p. 1156.
(3) *U. N. Treaty Series*, vol. 41, p. 72.
(4) Cf. *The Economist*, vol. 156, p. 62.

d. *China.* After the Communists came to power there was carried out extensive nationalization of private businesses in industry and commerce. In the event, however, the state enterprises that were established did not function particularly effectively. In 1953, therefore, these were denationalized, and the private businesses were once more carried on under their old names and under the direction of their former owners. The owners, however, came under the complete control of the state, both as regards fixing of prices, wages, and so on.

e. *Czechoslovakia.* On 27th October, 1945, Czechoslovakia passed a number of nationalization laws(1), as a result of which a great part of Czech industrial activity was taken over by the state(2).

The decrees issued in pursuance of the laws covered the mining industry and the more important branches of industry employing a specified number of workers(3), certain industrial undertakings within the food industry(4) banking business(5), and all insurance companies(6). At the end of 1947 these nationalization measures covered in all 8379 undertakings employing over 1 million persons, or 65 % of the total industrial capacity of the country.

The nationalization affected the interests of Czech nationals as well as those of foreigners. It is known, for example, that the nationalized American interests were estimated at $ 30—50 million(7).

All the nationalization decrees contain uniform provisions to the effect that compensation was to be paid to the owners of nationalized property, unless they were of German or Hungarian nationality, or had disloyally collaborated with the enemy. If as a result of these provisions a company was not entitled to compensation, the individual shareholders could nevertheless obtain compensation, if the said shareholders were not responsible for the circumstances that deprived the company of the right

---

(1) The 19th May, 1945, the Czech president issued a decree concerning the confiscation of "ownerless property", i. e. property belonging to German or Hungarian nationals or to Czechs who had treasonably collaborated with the enemy. The decree, motivated by penal considerations, can hardly be characterized as nationalization — all the more as directly after the confiscation the state sold the property to private individuals and companies. Cf. *Dep. St. Bul.*, vol. 15, (1946), p. 1028.

(2) Cf. Doman, *op. cit.*, p. 1143, and Oatman, "The Nationalization Program in Czechoslovakia", *Dep. St. Bul.*, vol. 15, (1946), p. 1027 ff.

(3) Decree No. 100/45.

(4) Decree No. 101/45.

(5) Decree No. 102/45.

(6) Decree No. 103/45.

(7) Oatman, *loc. cit.* Official American sources, however, in connection with the commencement of the Czecho—American Negotiations on Compensation, 28th November, 1955, state that the American claims are about $ 200 million.

to obtain compensation(1). This rule is of particular importance for foreign shareholders in nationalized companies.

In order to raise capital for the payment of compensation, a fund was set up, whose means were to come from the profits of the nationalized undertakings. Compensation was to be paid according to the value of the nationalized property, calculated on the basis of the official price level at the date when the law came into force, less company debt. Compensation was to be paid in bonds or — in special cases — in some other manner to be determined by the government.

A law of 15th May, 1946, however, introduced a tax on war profits and capital gains, with the result that the amounts of compensation promised would in any case be reduced essentially. So far no compensation has been paid to the nationals of the country under the nationalization decrees.

With special reference to foreign property the Czech government announced in January 1946, that compensation payments for nationalized property in which foreign capital was invested would be arranged through direct negotiation with the investors' governments, and that such compensation would be paid in the form of 3 % Government bonds. In part conformity with this declaration compensation has been paid to a certain extent, cf. infra Part III.

After President Gottwald came into power in March 1948, nationalization was continued. Nationalization took place with retroactive effect from 1st January, 1948(2) of wholesale trade, foreign trade, the building industry, travel agencies, and hotel and restaurant business.

f. *Egypt.* As a link in President Nasser's attempt to stabilize his régime and maintain the independence of Egypt of the Western World Decree Law No. 285 Respecting the Nationalization of the Universal Suez Maritime Canal Company was issued July, 26th, 1956.

Under section I of the law the nationalization comprized all money, rights and obligations of the company, and it was further provided that all organisations and committees operating the company are dissolved.

Concerning the problem of compensation it was said in the same provision:

> "Shareholders and holders of constituent shares shall be compensated in accordance to the value of the shares on the Paris Stock Market on the day preceding the enforcement of this law.
>
> Payment of compensation shall take place immediately the State receives all the assets and property of the nationalized company."

The nationalization of this international fairway caused the summoning of the above-mentioned conference in London in August 1956, which was attended by the eighteen greatest users of the canal.

---

(1) *Dep. St. Bul.*, vol. 15, (1946), p. 1003.
(2) The law was promulgated 2nd June, 1948.

g. *France.* Already in the last year of the war a nationalization of the most important industries commenced. By a law of 13th December, 1944, a public company for the exploitation of the coal mines of north-eastern France was established(1).

The law of 2nd December, 1945, nationalized the Banque de France and the four biggest commercial banks(2). This law was the consequence of a wish long nourished for government influence on the economy of the country and in particular on the policy of the Banque de France. The law is also remarkable for the restriction of scope, in that nationalization did not extend to all banks of a certain size, as some of the big banks (Banque de Paris des Pays-Bas and Union Parisienne), owned by foreign capital, were not nationalized. This was no doubt due to the fear of international political complications.

An equivalent reserve was not apparent in the case of the rest of the nationalization laws.

By the law of 26th June, 1945, all airway companies were absorbed by the state-owned Air France.

The law of 8th April, 1946, nationalized the electricity and gas undertakings. What decided whether a given undertaking was covered by the law was the size of the average production in a given specified number of years. Immediately after this — by a law of 25th April, 1946, two-thirds of the leading insurance companies were nationalized, and by the law of 17th May, 1946, the state took over the remaining privately owned coal mines.

In all these cases of nationalization the French government payed compensation in the form of Government bonds, paying 3 % per annum. The value of the nationalized property was fixed in the case of companies at a certain average quotation for the shares. In the case of the bank shares the value was fixed according to the exchange quotations at a time when rumours of nationalization had depressed the market. In this case the compensation can scarely be said to be full.

The law that nationalized the electricity and gas undertakings provides in Art. 13, last paragraph, that "the interests of foreign shareholders will be regulated according to special regulations issued by the ministers of production, foreign affairs and finance." In the course of the parliamentary debate on this law it emerged that the French government were willing to give greater compensation to foreigners than to their own nationals(3).

In addition to these cases of nationalization with a social-political basis there were a number of other activities, among others, the Renault Works, which were taken over by the state immediately after the war

(1) Doman, *op. cit.*, p. 1141.
(2) Myers, *op. cit.*, p. 189.
(3) Doman, *op. cit.*, p. 1142.

on the grounds that their owners had disloyally collaborated with the enemy. This taking over by the state was not accompanied — since it was of the nature of a penalty — by any compensation.

h. *Great Britain.* Immediately after the conclusion of the Second World War there was begun in Great Britain the nationalization of those branches of industry that were of greatest importance for export and for the conditions of the labour market.

As from 1st January, 1947, the British coal industry was nationalized in the main in order to rationalize and increase production(1). By an Act of 6th August, 1947, the whole of the British transport system(2) was nationalized affecting 1½ million employees, or 6½ % of the total British labour force.

All electricity undertakings were then nationalized by an Act of 13th August, 1947. This nationalization affected 570 companies to a value of around £ 370 million.

By an Act of 24th November, 1949, the British steel industry was nationalized. The Act affected 96 large concerns, and expressly excepted the American owned Ford Works at Dagenham. According to Schwarzenberger(3), this was on account of the recognition by Great Britain that in accordance with the rules of international law foreign property cannot be nationalized. This view was not supported in the Parliamentary debate on the question prior to the passing of the Act. Mr. G. R. Strauss, Minister of Supply, addressing the Standing Committee of the House of Commons on the question spoke as follows:

> "We felt that it would be unwise to use the Bill for the nationalization of steel as a method of nationalization of a very important part of the car industry. One of these days a Government may want to nationalize the motor car industries, but the right way will be to do it properly."

Mr. Strauss emphasized that this was the sole reason and expressly denied that it had anything whatever to do with the American shareholders(4).

All acts of nationalization in Great Britain took place against compensation. Compensation was paid in Government bonds, corresponding to the value of the nationalized property(5). The rate of interest on the

(1) In connection with the nationalization it was decided that around £ 200 million should be invested by the state in this industry for modernisation, new plant, etc. Cf. Tobin, "Nationalization in Great Britain — First Year", *Dep. St. Bul.*, vol. 15, (1948), p. 617.

(2) Cf. G. J. Walker, "The Transport Act 1947", *Economic Journal*, vol. 58, (1948), p. 11 ff.

(3) *British Property*, p. 310.

(4) *The Times*, 2nd February, 1949, p. 4, cf. also *The Times*, 28th January, 1949.

(5) Drucker, "Compensation for Nationalized British Property", *A. J. I. L.*, vol. 49, (1955), p. 477, states that at all events the amounts of compensation in connection with the Iron and Steel Act were considerably lower than the value of the nationalized property.

bonds was considerably lower than that previously received by the owners of the nationalized capital, but considering the security offered by the bonds they may be said to have amounted to full compensation.

It is characteristic of nationalization in Britain that the abolition of private ownership was not regarded even by the British Labour Party as in itself a desirable aim, but was in the main considered as a means to a better and more rational exploitation of technical resources(1).

i. *Holland.* By a decree dated 20th April, 1945, Holland nationalized the mining industry which had been badly hit by the war(2).

j. *Hungary.* Even before the nationalization laws of 1945 a large part of Hungarian industry and transport was under state ownership, and nationalization thus came merely as an extension of the desire of the state for control of the economic life of the country.

As from 1st January, 1946, the coal mines were nationalized together with their appurtenant power plants, carbide factories, etc. Later on in the same year the electricity undertakings were nationalized and certain parts of the food industry. On 30th November, 1946, heavy industry came under state control, but its nationalization did not take place till 25th March, 1948. At the same time there were also nationalized steam mills, breweries, dairy farms, oil installations, sugar factories, etc.

The banks together with the industrial concerns belonging to them were nationalized by a law of 24th July, 1947(3).

A general nationalization law was passed on 8th May, 1948. This nationalized all activities which at a given specified time had employed not less than 100 persons, together with activities which — irrespective of the number of employees — were of special importance(4). This law expressly provides (Section 11) that nationalization does not affect property belonging to foreign nationals or juridical persons situated outside the country, provided that the foreigners have acquired their property before 20th January, 1940.

The result of this provision was, inter alia, that oil production was not covered by the nationalization law, since all the oil fields in Hungary were American property. The importance of this, however, was reduced when the Hungarian Government by a decree No. 9960/1948 seized the

(1) This gave rise to severe Communist criticism. Thus, in an article in the Russian paper *New Times*, (1948), no. 28, p. 4 ff, Leonidan asserts under the headline "Shame Nationalization of the British Iron and Steel Industry", that the British "pseudo-nationalization is a swindle, aiming at protecting the capitalists against worse interference in order that the latter — as civil servants — may be in a position to exploit the workers further ...".

(2) Doman, *op. cit.*, p. 1142.

(3) *Dep. St. Bul.*, vol. 17, (1947), p. 430.

(4) Doman, *op. cit.*, p. 1152.

American oil companies on the grounds that they had shown themselves guilty of "economic sabotage"(1).

Exempt from nationalization were also activities acquired as a result of international argreements, in particular in pursuance of the Peace Treaty of 10th February, 1947.

The nationalization laws contained provisions for compensation, but these have not proved themselves effective.

k. *India.* On 1st July, 1955, there was carried out the nationalization of India's largest banking undertaking, The Imperial Bank of India. The nationalization involved the setting up of a state bank, in which, however, the former shareholders in Imperial Bank were permitted to keep 45 % of the total share capital of the state bank.

At the time of nationalization The Imperial Bank of India had branches in Pakistan, Burma, Ceylon and Great Britain. The problem of the transfer of these branches to state ownership has not been solved as yet.

On nationalization the owners received compensation. It is expected that further nationalization will take place.

l. *Iran.* In order to combat economic difficulties which had arisen after the Second World War, and to satisfy nationalistic elements in the Iranian population, the Iranian government attempted towards the end of 1949 to increase the revenue from the oil wells exploited by the British company, Anglo-Iranian Oil Company(2). This attempt was unsuccessful, and on 2nd May, 1951, the Iranian Shah signed a nationalization law covering the oil industry of the whole country. The law in its entirety reads as follows:

> "For the happiness and prosperity of the Iranian Nation and for the purpose of securing world peace, it is hereby resolved that the oil industry throughout all parts of the country without exception be nationalized; that is to say, all operations of exploration, extraction and exploitation shall be carried out by the Government."

At the same time the Shah signed regulations for the carrying out of the nationalization in so far as concerned the Anglo-Iranian Oil Company, which held the monopoly of the exploitation of the Iranian oil fields. These regulations set up a council to take over the entire activity of the company. It was determined that the Iranian government should deposit 25 % of the net receipts of the undertaking to cover any claims for compensation that might be made by the British company. Ford

(1) Cf. the American Note of Protest of 30th November, 1948, *Dep. St. Bul.*, vol. 19, (1948), p. 736.

(2) Cf. Alan W. Ford, *The Anglo-Iranian Oil Dispute of 1951—1952*, (1954), p. 51.

states(1) that the value of the Company's refinery at Abadan at the time of the nationalization was in the region of £ 250 million, to which must be added the value of the company's other assets which added up to a similar amount. Since in its last year the Company had had a total net profit of £ 84 million, the provision of the Iranian law concerning compensation will mean — provided that the nationalized company has the same earning capacity and opportunity as the Anglo-Iranian Oil Company — that full compensation, apart from interest, will at the earliest be paid in the course of about 24 years.

For the content of Great Britain's protest on the occasion of this nationalization, see infra under D.

m. *Jugoslavia.* Jugoslavia's nationalization law was passed 5th December, 1946. As the result of this law private activities of a specified size within 42 branches of industry were nationalized, including mines, the oil industry, transport, electricity, the food industry, banks, insurance companies, textiles and wholesale trade(2).

The nationalized property was to be compensated for by payment in Government bonds in proportion to the net value at the time of nationalization. However, compensation was not to be awarded to Germans or others who during the war had collaborated with the enemy. The burden of proof that such collaboration had in fact not taken place rested on the owners of the undertakings that had been nationalized. And not in Jugoslavia either have nationals of the country as yet received payment of compensation.

Jugoslavia has refused to pay individual compensation to foreign nationals, but has declared herself willing to conclude agreements with other governments, and for details of this cf. infra in Part III.

n. *Mexico.* The Mexican oil industry — owned by American, British and Dutch companies — was nationalized(3) by the President's decree of 18th March, 1938.

This decree was the final stage of a development which had begun in 1917, with the adoption of Mexico's new constitution. Art. 27 of this constitution stated that the ownership of the land and of the resources to be found in the land belonged to the state. On the authority of this pronouncement a law was passed in 1925, which aimed at certain restrictions upon the existing rights of foreign companies, which rights were to be superseded by concessions of limited duration. However, the oil companies disputed the constitutional validity of the law, and by a

(1) *Ibid.*, p. 188.
(2) *Dep. St. Bul.*, vol. 15, (1946), p. 1150.
(3) Cf. Gaither, *Expropriation in Mexico*, (1940), Woolsey, *op. cit.*, p. 519, and Friedman, *op. cit.*, p. 25 ff.

decision of the Supreme Court on 17th November, 1927, the oil companies' claim was upheld(1).

In 1936, however, the conflict about the foreign oil companies broke out again(2). The oil workers' union — presumably inspired by the government — put in exorbitant claims to the companies with regard to wages, holidays, social benefits, etc., and when the companies rejected these claims a general strike was called. The strike ended after a commission had been set up to investigate the financial capacity of the companies to grant the workers' claims. This investigation was unfavourable to the companies, but despite the fact that the Supreme Court in a decision of 1st March, 1938, ruled that the workers' claims must for the most part be met, the companies refused. Whereupon the President deemed himself entitled to issue the above-mentioned decree of nationalization(3).

The foreign states whose nationals and companies were affected by the nationalization protested to Mexico and demanded compensation. After negotiations that lasted for years this problem was settled by a treaty of agreement. Cf. for further details infra in Part III.

o. *New Zealand.* As from 1st April, 1949, the state took over the ownership of all located and unlocated coal deposits in New Zealand. In all cases where it was a question of coal mines that were being worked compensation was paid to the former owners. The amount of compensation was calculated on the basis of production in the years 1941—1947, and amounted normally to 15 times the average annual profit.

p. *Poland.* The Polish nationalization law of 3rd January, 1946(4), contains firstly, rules of a penal character, whereby all activities owned by the German Reich or by German nationals were nationalized without compensation (Art. II), and, secondly, rules whereby all other activities of a given specified character were to go over to state ownership (Art. III).

The activities covered by the general nationalization all belong to one of the 17 given specified branches of industry, including mines, the oil industry, water works, the iron and steel industry, the sugar industry,

---

(1) Cf. *Mexican Petroleum Company of California v. Secretary of Industry, Commerce and Labour,* (1927), *A. J. I. L.,* vol. 22, (1938), p. 421.

(2) Gaither, *op. cit.,* p. 52.

(3) Art. 1 of the decree reads as follows: "There are hereby declared expropriated, because of their being of public utility, and in favor of the Nation, the machinery, installations, buildings, pipelines, refineries, storage tanks, ways of communication, tank cars, distributing stations and all other real and personal property ... (belonging to 15 named companies)."

(4) Cf. Leon Goldberger-Laure Metzger, "The Polish Nationalization Law", *Dep. St. Bul.,* vol. 15, (1946), p. 651 ff., and Doman, *op. cit.,* p. 1146 ff.

breweries, yeast production, the textile industry, printing works, etc. In addition every activity was nationalized which employed more than 50 men per shift.

On 30th September, 1946, the Polish Government published a list of 513 firms which were confiscated without compensation in pursuance of Art. II of the law, and of 404 nationalized firms for which it was the intention of the Polish government to pay compensation. In both groups of firms alien property was extensively involved(1).

Art. VI of the law laid down that nationalization also covered all claims against the nationalized undertakings, apart from such as belonged to Polish public juridical persons, as well as all claims, licences, patents, etc. belonging to the activities.

According to Art. VII of the nationalization law, compensation was to be paid to the owners of activities nationalized in pursuance of Art. III, within one year after the amount of the compensation had been fixed. Just as in the Czech law, the compensation was to be paid in the form of Government bonds, or in quite exceptional circumstances in ready money or some other way. The amount of compensation was to be fixed by a special commission on lines indicated in fuller detail in the law(2).

With reference to these very detailed regulations concerning compensation, the Polish Minister of Industry, Hilary Minc, declared on Warsaw radio on 2nd January, 1946, that the whole nation stood behind him when he said that full compensation was to be paid in such measure, in such a form and in such circumstances, that it would not have the effect of handicapping the development of Poland's economy(3). Up to the time of writing no compensation has been paid as yet to Polish nationals or companies. Concerning compensation to aliens, see infra, in Part III.

q. *Roumania.* The first nationalization law was passed in Roumania on 28th December, 1947(4), and referred exclusively to the Roumanian National Bank. On 13th April, 1948, the Constitution of the Roumanian People's Republic provided authority for further nationalization(5), and nationalization was extended by the law of 11th June, 1948, to cover great parts of industry, mines, banks, insurance and transport.

A large part of Roumanian industry was in foreign hands(6), but these undertakings too were affected by the measures of nationalization. The law of 1948, however, contains two special provisions in so far as

(1) *Dep. St. Bul.*, vol. 15, (1946), p. 654.
(2) For this see infra in § 17.
(3) *Dep. St. Bul.*, vol. 15, (1946), p. 653.
(4) *Dep. St. Bul.*, vol. 16, (1947), p. 668.
(5) Cf. Guggenheim, *Annuaire*, vol. 43 I, (1950), p. 77, Doman, *op. cit.*, p. 1154, and *World Today*, vol. 5, (1949), no. 1, p. 7.
(6) Friedman, *op. cit.*, p. 48, mentions the figure of 24 %.

alien property is concerned. Art. 1 lays down that in activities established by agreement between a foreign state and the Roumanian government all property was to be nationalized that did not belong to one of the two states. The rule, which was inserted on the initiative of Soviet Russia, aims exclusively at protecting Soviet Russian property(1). Art. 5 contains the following provision:

> "Undertakings, or parts of such undertakings' capital, belonging to member states of the United Nations, who have acquired property in accordance with the Peace Treaty or as part of payment of compensation as a result of the war, are not covered by the present law and are not nationalized."

Doman(2) gives it as his opinion that we have here an example of a distinction being made in the law between private individuals and, on certain conditions, states, and this may be due to concern for the immunity of these states. This can, however, scarcely be assumed to be the decisive consideration. The explanation is rather that by the Peace Treaty of 10th February, 1947, Art. 24(3), Roumania had bound herself to pay compensation "or restoration" for all measures, including confiscation and control of property belonging to members of the United Nations, where these measures had been taken in the period 1st September, 1939 — 15th September, 1947. It was thus politically impossible for Roumania about one year later to nationalize the same property.

The Roumanian nationalization law, too, contains provisions that compensation to the former owners shall be paid in government bonds, to be redeemed according to a percentage fixed by the Finance Minister, with the aid of the annual profits of the nationalized activities. The bonds were to be non-transferable, non-negotiable and to carry no interest. The value of the compensation — which incidentally has not yet been paid to Roumania's own nationals — must accordingly be described as doubtful.

r. *Scandinavia.* None of the Scandinavian countries has up till now undertaken acts of nationalization. The idea, however, has been put forward.

In *Norway* Rjukans Faglige Samorganisasjon (trade union), on behalf of the organized workers at A/S Norsk Hydro, put forward an application to the Norwegian parliament on 21st May, 1919, asking for the socialization as soon as possible of the undertaking. This representation resulted in the appointment of a government commission to "consider the question of the socialization of the A/S Hydro works at Rjukan and other questions arising in that connection". The commissions' terms of reference were extended to include in general the effects of nation-

---

(1) Concerning the American protest in this connection see supra § 12 A.

(2) *Op. cit.*, p. 1140.

(3) *U. N. Treaty Series*, vol. 42, p. 52.

alization, and the commission issued its report 27th June 1924(1). The majority proposal was that "the question of socialization be left for further consideration . . ."(2). No nationalization has so far taken place.

In *Sweden* a public committee was appointed in 1920, with the task of "undertaking an inquiry into the suitability of and requirements for the transfer to public ownership or public control of natural resources and means of production which are of great importance to the economy of the country and the good of the community or otherwise might be thought to profit by being under the management of public organs." The committee which sat for a number of years, and whose report contained interesting surveys of similar problems in other countries, proved to be, however, of no practical importance. One of the reasons for this was — apart from the political situation — that by its financial and monetary policy and regulation of agricultural prices and conditions of production, etc., the state acquired an increased influence on the economic life of the country(3).

In *Finland* after the end of the Second World War the Popular Democratic Party raised the question of the nationalization of water power and the more important industries. In the early part of 1947 the parliamentary group of the Popular Democratic Party brought in a Bill for nationalization. It was met with strong opposition on the part of the non-socialist parties, but was nevertheless referred to a committee. The nationalization committee that was appointed issued a report on 31st March, 1950, concerning the nationalization of power stations, the telephone service, the tobacco industry, the sugar industry, ect. This report does not appear to have been put into practice.

s. *Soviet Russia.* As a consequence of the social revolution and of Marxist doctrine a number of nationalization laws were put into effect in Soviet Russia. By a decree of 26th October, 1917, private ownership of land was abolished. The decrees of 14th December, 1917 and 26th January, 1918, nationalized the Russian banks and established a state monopoly of banking business, and from May 1918 onwards considerable sections of industry were nationalized. The nationalization measures covered the property of Russian nationals as well as that of aliens. In no case was compensation paid to the former owners(4).

On the annexation of the Baltic states by Soviet Russia measures of nationalization were also applied to these territories, as, for example, in Esthonia, whose national paper for 23rd July, 1940 contained a decree concerning the nationalization of banks, industrial activities, mines and

---

(1) *Innstilling fra Socialiseringskomiteen angående socialiseringsspørgsmålet i almindelighet med bilag* (1924).

(2) *Ibid.*, p. 218.

(3) Cf. Tage Erlander. *Svensk Oppslagsbok*, vol. 26, (1953), p. 881.

(4) A review of Russian nationalization measures is to be found in Friedman, *op. cit.*, p. 17 ff.

transport concerns. These nationalizations, too, affected a number of foreign industrial concerns. In the Esthonian nationalization laws there were no provisions for compensation, and none has been paid to Esthonian nationals.

t. *Turkey.* By a decree of 21st July, 1938(1) an attempt was made to nationalize the Turkish cement industry. The reason for this step was that the cement factories (for the most part Danish and Belgian) were not able to satisfy the demand for cement during the peak months of building activity, and also that there was criticism of the price policy of the privately owned factories. It was accordingly decided that the Turkish State Bank should purchase the private factories and their stocks. The purchase price — including the payment to foreign shareholders — was to be paid in Turkish pounds, whose convertibility was subject to certain restrictions.

The idea of nationalization, however, was given up before it was put into effect, and a decree of 25 th May, 1939, abolished the nationalization regulations.

3. *Conclusion.* From the survey of national legislation and administrative practice given above it will appear that nationalization is employed as one means among many towards the solution of economic-political problems in countries differing widely as regards geographical position, form of government, and the ideological basis of the individual governments. The majority of the nationalization laws of the countries we have considered contain provisions concerning the liability of the nationalizing state to pay compensation to those affected by the nationalization, though payment to their own nationals has only taken place in those few countries whose economic system is in the main founded upon liberalist principles.

It further appears from the nationalization laws under consideration that the measures of nationalization in practically speaking all countries also applied to alien property. In those states where alien property was wholly or partly excepted from nationalization, this apparently was due to considerations of a practical nature (for example, the Ford Works in Great Britain) or of a political nature (for example, the foreign banks in France an the United Nations property in Roumania), and in particular was not due to the view that alien property cannot for legal reasons be nationalized.

Against this background it is inadmissible to maintain that, because certain states do not recognize nationalization in their national economic policy, there should exist a generally accepted international standard whose substance is that nationalization — whether ac-

(1) *Resmi Gazette*, no. 3965 of 21st July, 1938.

companied by compensation, as in certain liberalist countries, or not — is in conflict with international law as being incompatible with the minimum demands of civilization, so that the alien or the country of his nationality can oppose the nationalization and claim recovery of the property(1). An international standard is the expression of and is determined by the legal attitude of the states, and in consequence must be in agreement with the legal view held by the states at any given time. At a time when or in a field where there is no uniform legal view among the majority of the states that create the leading opinion, it must therefore be admitted that there is no international standard. The opposite view, i.e. an attempt — without reference to the existing legal attitude among the states — to give to international law a content determined by certain political theories or economic systems, is not only unrealistic, but also in conflict with the fundamental aims of the international legal system, viz., the regulation of co-operation among sovereign states with a view to avoiding conflict.

D. *The international interests of the states.*

The question can be raised as to whether, on the basis of an analysis of the interests conflicting in the event of the nationalization of alien property(2), it must nevertheless be assumed that nationalization of alien property without compensation cannot be considered as legally justified by reference to the territorial jurisdiction of a state. The fact mentioned above, that it was not due to legal considerations that a few individual states forbore to nationalize foreign property, does not necessarily preclude the view that nationalization of alien property is against international law. The denial of the existence of a legal restriction on the right of the states to nationalize alien property is no more than a conclusion drawn from official pronouncements, and it might well be imagined that governments, for example, out of respect for the principle of sovereignty that has been over-inflated in the national political debate, may not wish to admit publicly that the sovereign right to legislate is subject to international limitations.

A preferential legal position for aliens, beyond what might follow from general maxims of justice and the rule of the minimum demands of civilization, may be based on the wish of the states to

(1) Doman thinks otherwise, *op. cit.*, p. 1136.
(2) Cf. supra §§ 3 and 4.

secure to their nationals in foreign countries a different and better legal position than in their own contry. In this case the state in question, in order to achieve this end, must also — on the basis of the legal reciprocity discussed in § 5 — allow foreigners a correspondingly favourable position. A situation of this nature occurs, inter alia, with regard to the international rule of exemption of aliens from military service. Military service is compatible with any international standard, but the wish of states that their nationals should not do military service in foreign countries has led to the international legal rule on the matter.

The question, therefore, is whether there may be among the states special reasons that create the desire that the property of their nationals in foreign countries — as distinct from property in their own country — shoul be excempted from nationalization.

Such a wish is hardly traceable.

An affirmative answer would lead to the economically and politically impossible situation that the nationals of a country, for fear of nationalization in their own country and confident that their own country would not tolerate nationalization in foreign countries, would place their investments abroad. The non-nationalized undertakings in a given country then would to a very large extent be based on foreign capital and open to foreign influence. This, particularly in international unsettled periods, might cause so great difficulties that it must be considered overwhelmingly improbable that the states should aim at creating a situation of this kind.

The economic interest of states in protecting the part of the national wealth that is invested abroad, does not necessarily require nationalization to be regarded as conflicting with international law, since this interest can be satisfied by an international liability to pay compensation in case of nationalization, cf. on this subject below in Part III.

The decisive factor for the legality of measures of nationalization must therefore be a balancing of the interest of the states in the widest possible unlimited territorial jurisdiction and their interest in protecting property abroad belonging to their nationals. Since, as has been stated, the latter interest in relation to the free exercise of territorial jurisdiction is of minor importance, the result consequently must be that nationalization affecting aliens — from the point of view of international law — is a legitimate expression of the jurisdiction of the state, and the home country of an alien affected by the nationalization so cannot enforce recovery or compel damages as against the nationalizing state.

The view maintained here is in accordance with the most modern international practice as regards nationalization.

Thus, when the American Government in a Note of 7th September, 1948, protested to the Roumanian Government against the nationalization by Roumania of American, but not of Soviet Russian, property, the United States expressly recognized the sovereign right of a state in general to nationalize foreign property. The Note runs:

> "While the United States Government has consistently recognized the right of a sovereign power to expropriate property subject to its jurisdiction and belonging to American nationals, the United States has likewise refused to recognize the validity of such expropriations in cases where they are discriminatory by nature and effect..."(1).

The view that nationalization is a legitimate interference, even if affecting alien property was evinced even more clearly in the Anglo-Iranian dispute concerning the Anglo-Iranian Oil Company:

After the Iranian Parliament had on 30th April, 1951, passed the law of nationalization of the oil industry, but before this law was promulgated on 2nd May, 1951, the British Foreign Secretary, Mr. Herbert Morrison, said in the House of Commons:

> "We do not of course dispute the right of a Government to acquire property in their own country...".

This view, which probably was dictated by the hope of a settlement of the affairs of the Anglo-Iranian Oil Company by negotiation, however, was maintained by the British Government throughout the entire course of the dispute.

Nor did the appeal by Great Britain of 26th May, 1951, to the Permanent Court of International Justice contain any assertion to the effect that the nationalization was contrary to internatitonal law, but only expressed the view that "*the carrying into effect* of the Iranian nationalization laws, to the extent that these aimed at a unilateral annulment of the 1933 concession, would be a violation of international law..."(2). This interpretation of the British claim was confirmed by the following statement made by Mr. Herbert Morrison in the House of Commons on 29th May, 1951:

(1) Cf. *Dep. St. Bul.*, vol. 19, (1948), p. 408. Although the Note employs the term expropriation, its relevance in this connection cannot be disputed, since the Note was occasioned by the Roumanian nationalization law.

(2) Cf. *Anglo-Iranian Oil Co. case (Jurisdiction)*, I.C.J. Reports (1952), p. 95.

> "Moreover, as His Majesty's Ambassador in Teheran has informed the Persian Government, while His Majesty's Government cannot accept the right of the Persian Government to repudiate contracts they are prepared to consider a settlement which would involve some form of nationalization, provided — a consideration to which (the United Kingdom Government) attach some importance — it were satisfactory in other respects."

When the negotiations between Great Britain and Iran had come to nothing in the first instance, and after the Permanent Court of International Justice on 5th July, 1951, had ordered "provisional measures" to be introduced so that the position of the parties should not be prejudiced, the British Government on 29th July, 1951, handed a Note to the Iranian Government, in which the British view was once more confirmed(1):

> "His Majesty's Government recognize on their own behalf, and on that of the Company, the principle of the nationalization of the oil industry in Iran . . .".

Finally, it may be stated that similar views were advanced by most of the states which took part in the London Conference of August 1956 in the discussion on the Egyptian nationalization of the Suez Maritime Canal Company.

E. *Must nationalization in defiance of contractual obligations be regarded as contrary to international law?*

During the debate — mentioned in § 2 supra — at the Institut de Droit Internationale, held in 1952 on subject of the international effects of nationalization, the question was discussed whether nationalization must be regarded as contrary to international law if it was effected in defiance of contractual obligations undertaken by the nationalizing state towards foreign nationals(2). A resolution to this effect was rejected, however.

This result prima facie may seem preposterous. It is felt as a positive violation of the general sense of justice that a state should be free to annul a promise that was given in the form of a contract, whereas a similar promise forming part of a treaty is in principle inviolable on the grounds of the maxim *pacta sunt servanda*. The distinction between rights based on contract and rights based on treaty seems particularly crude when it is borne in mind that it will often depend upon a politically or economically fortuitous situa-

(1) Ford, *op. cit.*, p. 102.
(2) *Annuaire*, vol. 44 II (1952), p. 305—319.

tion whether a right is assured to a foreign state — or to a foreign company which in the main is based on state interests — by virtue of a treaty or a concession.

Nevertheless it must be accepted that the view which found expression in the vote described above in the Institut de Droit Internationale is in accordance both with the doctrine of international law and with international practice. The fact that nationalization normally is not a breach of international law cannot be altered by the fact that nationalization destroys contractual rights, for example, a concession which the nationalizing state has granted to a foreign national or foreign company. The contract must be regarded as giving a title to a legal status in municipal law, and the obligation of the state to maintain such status must be based on municipal law and not on international law(1). The breach of the contractual rights of the private party to the contract involved by the nationalization consequently cannot be a breach of international law, but on the other hand may cause remedies to be employed on the grounds of breach of the municipal rules of contract.

It must be this view that underlies the statement made in connection with the conclusion between Sweden and Poland of the treaty of 16th November, 1945, concerning compensation for the nationalization of Swedish property, to the effect that the claims of Svenska Tändstiksaktiebolaget, originating from the concession agreement with Poland of 17th November, 1930, rested on a special legal basis(2) as compared with claims based upon the nationalization of non-contractual rights of property.

There is no rule in international law that gives a greater degree of protection to rights secured by contract than to other rights of property(3).

---

(1) Rolin, *op. cit.*, p. 313, Guggenheim, *op. cit.*, p. 315.

(2) Cf. *Kunglig Majestäts Proposition* nr. 187 (1950), p. 12 ff. Cf. also the *Case of Delagoa Bay and East African Railway Company* (1891), where compensation for annulment of a concession which Portugal had granted to an American national was determined according to the rules of civil law governing liability for breach of contract, see Whiteman, *Damages in International Law,* (1932), vol. III, p. 1694 and 1697; Fischer—Williams, *loc. cit.*, p. 3.

(3) In connection with the international debate on the occasion of the Egyptian nationalization of the Suez Maritime Canal Company it was not possible to uphold the view that the Egyptian action was contrary to international law because Egypt had violated he Canal Company's concession that was to last until the year 1967.

PART III: COMPENSATION

§ 13.
INTRODUCTION

The examination of the subject so far has led to the conclusion that the nationalization of foreign property is legal in itself in international law, unless it is a case of nationalization of state-owned property used in official government service, or the nationalization is in breach of the provisions of a treaty, or it constitutes a violation of the formal principle of equality. On the other hand nationalization raises the question whether a nationalization that is lawful in itself involves a liability in international law for the nationalizing state to pay compensation to the foreigner who is affected by it.

If this question is answered in the affirmative the result will be that non-payment of compensation — but not the nationalization in itself — must be regarded as a breach of international law. In that case it must be possible to obtain judgment for compensation, and to employ reprisals or other lawful measures to enforce the law against the state that has not complied its liability to pay compensation.

§ 14.
DOES NATIONALIZATION ENTAIL A LIABILITY IN INTERNATIONAL LAW TO PAY COMPENSATION?

A. *Traditional views.*

The legal opinon on this question is not unanimous.

The international legal opinon — that is supported on a legal practice as regards the protection of vested rights that is by no means uniform — largely assumes(1) that the compulsory aquisition

(1) Cf. for example, Borchard, *op. cit.*, p. 184, Bullington, "Problems of International Law in the Mexican Constitution of 1917", *A.J.I.L.*, vol. 21, (1927), p. 685, Hyde, "Compensation for Expropriation", *A.J.I.L.*, vol. 33, (1939), p. 112, Shawcross, *Some Problems of Nationalization* (1954), and Joseph, *International Aspects of Nationalization*, (1954).

of property entails a liability to give adequate, prompt and effective compensation.

This view, however, implies that the situation in question makes payment of compensation not only reasonable, i. e., in agreement with the basic principles of law, but also that it is within the bounds of possibility(1). In this connection it must be recalled that the Iranian nationalization of the Anglo-Iranian Oil Company at an estimate involved assets amounting to about $ 1400 million(2), whereas the Iranian gold reserve — which constituted the main part of Iran's liquid national wealth — at the time of the nationalization only amounted to $ 239 millions(3).

A demand for adequate, prompt and effective compensation in such a situation would be absurd unless it were interpreted as implying that a state, which — like Iran — lacked the economic possibilities to make such compensation payments — should refrain from nationalization(4). Such an interpretation of the rules of international law would be difficult to uphold because the interests mentioned in the foregoing motivating the acts of nationalization are far too important to allow such interpretation. This point of view was formulated clearly by General Don Eduardo Hay, the Mexican Foreign Minister, in a Note of 3rd August, 1938, to the United States Ambassador in connection with the Mexican agricultural expropriations. The problem raised by Mexico in connection with these expropriations is, however, just as applicable in case of nationalization. This Note says inter alia:

> "The political, social, and economic stability and the peace of Mexico depend on the land being placed anew in the hands of the country people who work it; therefore, its distribution, which implies the transformation of the country, that is to say, the future of the nation, could not be halted by the impossibility of paying immediately the value of the properties belonging to a small number of foreigners who seek only a lucrative end.
>
> On the one hand, there are weighed the claims of justice and the improvement of a whole people, and on the other hand, the purely pecuniary interests of some individuals. The position of

(1) Cf. Bindschedler, *op. cit.*, p. 39.

(2) According to Ford, *op. cit.*, p. 188—189.

(3) Cf. *Review of Economic Conditions in the Middle East*, (1951), p. 76, published by the United Nations Secretariat.

(4) Cf. Hyde, *op. cit.*, p. 112, who demands the return of the property to the former owners if the nationalizing state cannot pay; similarly Woolsey, *op. cit.*, p. 526 and Verziil, *Annuaire*, vol. 44, II, (1952), p. 265, where reference is made to the acceptance of this solution by the Indonesian Government in a parliamentary debate on nationalization.

Mexico in this unequal dilemma could not be other than the one she has assumed, and this is not stated as an excuse for her actions but as a true justification thereof".(1)

As the result of the view that the liability to pay adequate, prompt and effective compensation in case of nationalization would render such nationalization impracticable or defeat the ends of it, La Pradelle(2) maintains that the liability to pay compensation normally entailed by the compulsory acquisition of foreign property in the case of nationalization must be reduced to compensation fixed unilaterally by the nationalizing state. Other outhorities, however, go even further, and firmly say that there ought to be no claim for compensation in case of nationalization.

Despite the apparently logical conclusions in these views it must, nevertheless, be maintained that they are not compatible with existing international practice.

B. *Practice.*

1. *Treaties.* An investigation of the most modern international treaties shows that the view that the nationalization of foreign property entails a liability for the nationalizing state to pay compensation is apparently confirmed by a number of bilateral treaties:

Bulgaria has concluded treaties(3) with:

Great Britain	20.9.1955
Norway	2.12.1955
Switzerland	26.11.1954

Czechoslovakia has concluded treaties with(4):

Belgium	19.3.1947	30.9.1952
France	6.8.1948	2.6.1950
Great Britain	28.9.1949	
Holland	4.11.1949	
Sweden	15.3.1947	
Switzerland	18.12.1946	22.12.1949
U. S. A.	14.11.1946	

(1) Cf. Briggs, *op. cit.*, (1953), p. 558.

(2) *Annuaire,* vol. 43 I, (1950), p. 128.

(3) The term treaties is taken here and in the following in the widest sense, covering every form of international agreement. Where more than one date is given this means that the earlier agreement entered into between the parties was subsequently superseded by the later one, cf. *infra* § 15.

(4) Negotiations with Denmark have been commenced. On 28. 11. 1955 negotiations were also commenced with U. S. A.

France has concluded treaties with(1):

Belgium	18.2.1949(2)	
Great Britain	11.4.1951	
Switzerland	21.11.1949	

Hungary has concluded treaties with(3):

Belgium/Luxemburg ..	1.2.1955	
France	12.6.1950	
Sweden	26.7.1946	31.3.1951
Switzerland	19.7.1950	

Jugoslavia has concluded treaties with(4):

France	14.4.1951
Great Britain	23.12.1948
Italy	23.5.1949
Sweden	12.4.1947
Switzerland	27.9.1948
Turkey	5.1.1950
U. S. A.	19.7.1948

Mexico has concluded treaties with:

Great Britain	7.2.1946
Holland	7.2.1946
U. S. A.	29.9.1943

Poland has concluded treaties with(5):

Denmark	5.12.1947	12.5.1949	26.2.1953
France	19.3.1948		
Great Britain	24.1.1948	14.1.1949	11.11.1954
Norway	4.2.1948	23.12.1955	
Sweden	28.2.1947	26.11.1949	
Switzerland	25.6.1949		
U. S. A.	24.4.1946	27.12.1946	

(1) Treaty propably also concluded with Holland and Canada.

(2) With amendments dated 20th March, 1950.

(3) Negotiations with Great Britain were commenced 15. 9. 1955. Negotiations with Denmark have also been commenced.

(4) Treaty probably concluded with Belgium. In September, 1955, negotiations on compensation were commenced with Hungary. For political reasons these negotiations, however were discontinued the 23th September, 1955, and no result was achieved.

(5) According to Polish sources a treaty was also concluded with Belgium.

Roumania has concluded a treaty with:

Switzerland	3.8.1951	

Soviet Russia has concluded a treaty with(1):

Sweden	30.5.1941	7.10.1946

2. *What motives lead a nationalizing state to conclude treaties respecting compensation?* The provisions contained in these treaties will be surveyed in the following pages, but an attempt will be made here to decide whether the said treaties can be regarded as the expression of a general rule in international law to the effect that nationalization directed against foreigners entails a liability to pay compensation, or whether the treaties are an expression of special favour, or may be dictated by special circumstances, so that the said treaties afford no proof of the existence of a general rule of international law. It might even be asked if it is warrantable *e contrario* to conclude from the said treaties that there is no such rule in general international law.

Apparently the treaties must be interpreted on the background of special circumstances. The list of states entitled to compensation shows that the latter largely are great powers or states on which the compensating state is to a certain extent dependent financially or commercially.

An inquiry into the treaties with a view to determining the motives that may have influenced the nationalizing states to promise compensation affords an extremely varied picture:

a. *Force.* The position often is that the nationalizing state is in a state af dependence, and as a result has no choice of paying or refusing to pay compensation.(2) The treaty between the United States and Jugoslavia of 19th July, 1948(3) e. g. came into existence in a situation where the United States government — at a time when Jugoslavia was in great need of foreign exchange — had re-

(1) Concerning property in the Baltic States. Negotiations with Denmark were commenced in March 1957.

(2) Cf. also the agreement between the United States and Soviet Russia in 1933 concerning compensation for the nationalization of American property in Russia (the Litvinov-Agreement). The agreement was a necessary condition for the diplomatic recognition which Russia was at this time anxious to obtain.

(3) *Dep. St. Bul.*, vol. 19, (1948), p. 137 and 139.

fused the specific request of Jugoslavia to release a gold reserve belonging to Jugoslavia until compensation was paid for nationalized American property in Jugoslavia. The gold, that had been deposited in the United States at the beginning of the Second World War, amounted to $ 46,800,000,(1) and had originally been blocked to prevent Germany, or a satelite Jugoslav government dependent on Germany, from disposing of these assets. So there never was any doubt that the gold belonged to the Jugoslav government, and that the American government's refusal to release the gold was motivated exclusively by the coercion that might thereby be applayed against the nationalizing state.

b. *Release of frozen accounts.* An examination of treaty practice shows that agreements providing for compensation for nationalized property is often connected with release of accounts blocked by the claimant state. It will often be a question of comparatively small accounts, so that already the amount involved precludes any question of coercion on the part of the claimant state. In some cases the title of the nationalizing state to the blocked amounts has been disputed, and the doubt existing as to this question then has been disposed of in connection with the compensation agreements.

Release of blocked accounts has been carried through in connection with the compensation treaties between Great Britain and Jugoslavia, 23rd December, 1948, between Switzerland and Roumania, 3rd August, 1951, and Czechoslovakia, 22nd December, 1949, and Bulgaria, 26th November, 1954, and between Norway and Bulgaria, 2nd December, 1955, and Poland, 23rd December, 1955.

c. *Remission of debts.* The question of compensation from Poland for the loss of Danish property and Danish interests as a result of the Polish nationalization Law of 3rd January, 1946, and others, was first raised by Denmark under the Dano-Polish trade negotiations in 1947. As a consequence Denmark was accorded most favoured nation treatment by Poland in respect of Danish claims for compensation. This, however, was not effective, and in the period 18th November — 16th December, 1948 representatives of the governments of the two countries carried on negotiations concerning payment of compensation.(2) These negotiations resulted in the

(1) Cf. Rubin, *op. cit.*, p. 463. For comparison, the compensation amounted to the sum of $ 17,000,000.

(2) At the same time trade relations were discussed, resulting in the agreement of 14th December, 1948, on payments and exchange of goods, cf. *Lovtidende* C, (1949), p. 257.

Danish-Polish Protocol no. 1, signed in Warsaw on 12th May, 1949(1). In this Protocol the Polish government declared itself willing to pay compensation for Danish property and other interests which Poland had nationalized. On the other hand the Protocol also contained a provision to the effect that Denmark should remit an amount of Danish kr. 110.725, the balance of an assistance credit established after the First World War to assist new and war-damaged states.

A similar remission of claims against the Polish government was made by Sweden by the Swedish-Polish Compensation-Treaty of 16th November, 1949(2). The balance of the Swedish claim in respect of the assistance credit amounted to Swedish kr. 1.293,600.(3)

The agreement concluded between Great Britain and Poland on 11th November, 1954, contained provision to the effect that Poland's debt for the costs of the occupation of the plebiscite area in Upper Silesia etc., and Poland's debt in respect of the assistance credit should likewise be extinguished on the conclusion of the compensation agreement.(4)

Finally it may be mentioned that on the conclusion of the treaty of compensation between Norway and Poland on 23rd December, 1955, it was agreed by an exchange of Notes that Norway should remit Poland's debt in respect of the assistance credit given by Norway. According to the Norwegian Paliament's proposition of 22nd September, 1955,(5) this debt amounted to Norwegian kr. 4.379,430 and £ 386-5-0. It will be seen that this was a very considerable amount compared with the amount of compensation which Poland was to pay for nationalized Norwegian assets, viz., about 3—3½ million Norwegian kr.

d. *Commercial advantages.* Frequently compensation agreements are, however, dictated by considerations of commercial policy. This particularly is the case on the conclusion of a treaty of compensation simultaneous with the conclusion of a commercial treaty that gives the state allowing compensation specially favourable conditions.

So the compensation agreement concluded between Great Britain and Czechoslovakia on 28th September, 1949(6) which provided

(1) Cf. *Lovtidende* C, (1949), p. 567.
(2) Cf. *S. Ö.*, 1950, p. 925.
(3) Cf. the correspondance in connection with the compensation agreement, *ibid.*
(4) Cf. *T. S.*, no. 77, (1954).
(5) No. 103, (1955), p. 4.
(6) Cf. *T. S.*, No. 60, (1949).

that Czechoslovakia should pay a total sum of £ 8 million in compensation, refers in its preamble to the trade and finance treaty(1) concluded on the same date between the parties, wherein Great Britain promised to permit imports from Czechoslovakia of "non-essential" goods to an annual amount of £ 5,750,000

Similar methods were employed by Great Britain when obtaining compensation from Jugoslavia in pursuance of the compensation agreement concluded on 23rd December, 1948, which in Art. 1, where the amount of the compensation is fixed at £ 4,500,000, states that the payment "... shall be agreed between the Contracting Governments during the negotiations for a long-term trade agreement which shall be entered into at an early date".(2) 10% of the amount of compensation, however, was to be paid immediately in frozen Jugoslav assets which were released by an agreement concluded between the parties on the same day.(3)

On 28th February, 1947, Sweden and Poland signed a Protocol concerning the interests of Swedish physical and juridical persons in Poland, whereby Poland agreed to pay compensation to those affected by nationalization.(4) On 18th March, 1947, the same states concluded a treaty concerning the regulation of trade between them,(5) with a supplementary agreement concerning the part to be played by Sweden in the rebuilding of Polish industry in return for supplies of Polish coal and coke. This latter agreement contains provisions concerning credits and loans to Poland(6) and had for its purpose to secure to Poland the supply of very essential goods. The fact that despite the difference in dates there is a close connection between the trade and credit agreement and the compensation agreement appears from the following communication dated 18th March, 1947, from the head of the Polish delegation to the head of the Swedish delegation:

> "...With reference to the Protocol signed on 28th February, 1947, in Warsaw by representatives of the Swedish and Polish Governments concerning the interests of Swedish physical and juridical persons in Poland, ... I have the honour to confirm that my Government is prepared to bring the same into force ...

---

(1) Cf. *T. S.*, No. 62, (1949).
(2) Cf. *T. S.*, No. 2, (1949).
(3) Cf. *T. S.*, No. 3, (1949).
(4) Cf. *S. Ö.*, 1947, p. 131.
(5) Cf. *S. Ö.*, 1947, p. 95.
(6) Cf. art. IV, *loc. cit.*, p. 118.

I also wish to add, that in the discussions which in pursuance of this Protocol is to take place between the proper Polish authorities and Swedish physical and juridical claimants, the Polish Government will take into consideration the part played by Sweden provided for in the Agreement signed this day."(1)

This compensation agreement was, as a matter of fact, replaced by the treaty of 16th November, 1949, whereby Poland undertook to pay to Sweden a total of 116 million Swedish kr. by way of lump-sum compensation. Simultaneously an agreement was entered into respecting fresh credits to Poland and — as stated above — the remission of the assistance credit.

An agreement was concluded between France and Poland on 19th March, 1948(2), whereby Poland was to pay to France compensation for nationalized property by supplying a total of 3,800,000 tons of coal at $ 15 per ton, and this agreement too was linked with an agreement to the effect that France was to grant Poland credit corresponding to 50% of the compensation.

This direct connection between compensation agreements and trade agreements that give a special favour to the paying state has been used successfully by countries which — like Switzerland, for example — had a very favourable position in the international market in the period following on the Second World War.

But even where the compensation agreement is not directly coupled with a trade agreement that gives special favour to the paying state the motives for concluding treaties of compensation still can often be found in considerations of commercial policy. While the agreements concluded between Denmark and Poland concerning exchange of goods and payments do not contain or imply any liability for Denmark to import "non-essential" goods, or any Danish undertaking to grant special credits to Poland, the very fact that Poland undertook to pay a total of kr. 5.500,000 in compensation over a period of 15 years(3) through appropriation for that purpose of 0·5% of Poland's export to Denmark, implies that Poland can expect that until the compensation payments have been carried through there will be Polish exports to Denmark to a rather considerable extent compared with the total compensation.

Payment of compensation out of an export surplus is a feature in a very large number of compensation agreements. By way of example reference is made to the agreements between Switzerland

(1) *Loc. cit.*
(2) *Journal officiel* for 11th November, 1951.
(3) Cf. Protocol No. 2 of 26th February, 1953, *Lovtidende* C, (1954), p. 1.

and Czechoslovakia of 22nd December, 1949, between France and Czechoslovakia of 2nd June, 1950, between Sweden and Hungary of 31st March, 1951, and all compensation treaties concluded by Bulgaria.

On the basis of a review of the ascertainable circumstances in connection with the conclusion of compensation treaties it can be said with certainty that — in the absence of powerful means of coercion — there will nearly always be an incitement in the form of some special commercial-political advantages influencing the nationalizing state to pay compensation.(1)

3. *Discussion.* The above mentioned circumstances attending the conclusion of treaties of compensation do not, however, necessarily preclude these treaties being an expression of a rule of international law regarding a liability to pay compensation to foreigners affected by nationalization. The blocking of assets, the cessation or restriction of trade relations and credits(2), the refusal of diplomatic recognition, unfriendly political attitude, etc. as the case may be, may merely be expressing that the general — and not least the practical — means of upholding international law are applied to enforce legitimate claim for compensation against an unwilling party.

The fact that compensation in the main is paid to Great Powers or powers of great ecconomic significance to the nationalizing state cannot be taken to imply lack of legal basis for the liability to pay compensation, since those states usually have the largest share in the nationalized property and so the greatest interest in obtaining compensation, just as it is precisely such states that are able to enforce their claims.

The fact that the liability to pay compensation has hitherto been established exclusively by bi-lateral treaties cannot justify any conclusion to the effect that there is no general liability in international law to pay compensation. The economic problems involved in the payment of compensation are so complicated and diversified in

---

(1) In connection with the compensation negotiations initiated between the United States and Czechoslovakia on 28th November, 1955, the United States declared that the Americans for their part were firmly determined to oppose the Czech attempts to make the negotiations that had begun depend on questions that did not stand in a direct relation to claims for compensation.

(2) The state which is entitled to compensation will often announce, for example, that it does not wish to begin trade negotiations until the nationalizing state admits its willingness to pay compensation to those affected by the nationalization.

respect of the various states, that a general liability without individual details scarcely would be of any practical significance. This is true not only in respect of the fixation of the amount of compensation, but also in respect of the form in which payment is to be made and in respect of the currency problems involved. An international court, or a court of arbitration, would scarcely be suited to decide all these questions in a manner satisfactory to both parties.

The fact that the party entitled to compensation may grant credit or even loans to the party liable to pay compensation is no unknown feature in national law, e. g., the numerous credit arrangements where creditors grant considerable financial support to an insolvent debtor and so to enable the creditors, for example through continued business connection, to cover their losses. There is no justification for concluding from the granting of such credit that the creditors' original claims lacked legal foundation.

C. *Conclusion.*

It must be admitted, nevertheless, that it is not possible solely on the basis of international treaty practice to give a definite answer to the question whether lawful nationalization entails a liability to pay compensation to the victime of the same in case they are nationals of a foreign state. Treaty practice up till now has not been extensive enough, and in some respects has been too special in character, to be a basis for a decisive attitude to this question. With this reservation in mind, it may be maintained, however, that the recent development in the rules of international law in respect of nationalization seems to be tending towards a rule involving liability to pay compensation to foreigners affected by nationalization.

In the first place the correctness of this view seems to find support in the fact that in the municipal legislation of some countries (for example, in France) it is provided — presumably to comply with a legal obligation — that foreigners have a claim to a special legal position with regard to compensation for nationalized property, irrespective of the fact that the country's own nationals receive different and less favourable treatment.

And secondly, practical considerations — determined by the international interests of the countries — seems to give support to an unqualified liability to pay compensation in the case of nationalization of foreign property.

Despite the fact that almost all nationalization laws contain regulations to the effect that compensation *ought to be paid*(1), it must be admitted that national practice in most countries nationalizing private property seems to indicate that nationalization does not entail a liability to pay compensation to private citizens affected by the nationalization; but is must be assumed that this legal view in national practice has reference only to the nationalizing country's own nationals and is not applicable in international relations. This is due to the fact that the practical considerations behind nationalization will lead to different results in the national and in the international sphere as far as regards the problem of compensation. In the national sphere these practical considerations involve a wish to take over the citizens' property to the widest possible extent without compensation. In the international sphere however, the economic views will favour a rule involving liability to pay compensation. This is obvious as regards creditor-nations as such nations are interested in favouring a rule that will protect their own interests and those of their nationals abroad. As regards debtor-nations it might seem as if they would be interested in being able to nationalize foreign property without paying compensation, but a close consideration of their economic interests shows that a far-sighted economic policy must favour a rule under which nationalization of foreign property involves liability to pay compensation. Typical capital importing countries will — indirectly — improve their economy by the recognition of such a rule, even though compensation is not made to the country's own nationals, since such recognition of the duty to pay compensation to aliens will afford some protection for the foreign capital invested in that country. In the absence of such protection there is a serious risk that no foreign state or no foreign citizen would invest the capital that such country may need. The paradoxical situation that a country at the same time nationalizes foreign property and also tries to persuade foreign countries and their nationals invest in, for example, technical installations for the

---

(1) As a supplement to the account in § 12 above of national practice it can be stated that the Polish Minister for Industry etc. in the course of the discussion of the nationalization laws in the Polish National Council made the following statement:

"The confiscation of industrial property without compensation would mean embarking on the road of social revolution. This is not our road, and we are, therefore, carrying out nationalization with compensation in common with Czechoslovakia, France, and Britain ..." Hilary Minc, *The Nationalization of Industry in Poland*, (1946), p. 26.

development of the natural resources of the country could not exist for any length of time. The carrying out of such projects presupposes confidence in the economic systems of the countries in question. In order to create such long-term confidence in their capital market these capital-importing countries will be interested in giving compensation. So a rule to the effect that nationalization of foreign property involves a liability to pay compensation will be in the mutual interests of all states.

In this connection it is of the utmost importance to show that the said views evidently appear to have found expression in the practice of the states, for also the states whose economic policy is based on socialist theory, and who nationalize their own citizens' property without compensation, demand compensation in case of foreign nationalization of property belonging to their nationals. In this connection reference can be made to the fact that in the autumn of 1955 negotations were commenced between Hungary and Jugoslavia, in which both these countries demanded compensation for nationalization of property belonging to their nationals in the other state. *Socialistic development in national policy so apparently has not brought about the international result, that the states in question have relinquished claim for compensation in respect of nationalization in other countries.*

In the third place, with a wiew to the fact that in many cases treaties have been concluded providing for compensation to foreign nationals, both by capital-importing and capital-exporting states which nationalize the property of their own citizens without compensation, it must in the end be accepted that this policy is conducing to the creation — or the confirmation of — the international legal maxim that the nationalization of foreign property involves liability for the nationalizing state to pay compensation.

If this tendency in international law may be found correct it will be of importance to undertake an analysis of the pertinent treaties, in order thereby to find out what shall be considered most practical in the view of the states with regard to the substance of the liability to pay compensation in international law.

§ 15.
FORM OF COMPENSATION

In the cases where nationalizing states do not in their national law recognize a liability to pay full compensation to foreign nationals affected by the nationalization, and where, the foreign nationals cannot by application to the administrative organs of the nationalizing state, their courts, etc., enforce their claim without intervention from their respective home countries, the following forms of bilateral compensation treaties have so far been used:

A. Agreements in general terms.
B. Agreements providing for direct individual compensation.
C. Agreements providing for indirect individual compensation.
D. Agreements providing for global (lump-sum) compensation.

A. *Agreements in general terms.*

1. *Practice.* An agreement promising compensation for nationalized property in general terms was entered into by the United States and Czechoslovakia by an exchange of Notes dated 14th November, 1946.(1) The agreement, which was made in connection with discussions in Washington on the trade relations of the two states, etc., in chapter 7 contains the following provision:

> "The Government of the United States and the Government of Czechoslovakia will make adequate and effective compensation to nationals of one country with respect to their rights or interests in properties which have been or may be nationalized or requisitioned by the Government of the other country. In this connection, the Government of the United States has noted with satisfaction that negotations concerning compensation on account of such claims will shortly begin in Praha."

A similar agreement was concluded between the United States and Poland by an exchange of Notes on 24th April, 1946, in connection with negotations concerning a loan of about $ 40 million to Poland.(2)

The agreements under consideration here, whereby the nationalizing state pledges itself to pay compensation to foreign nationals affected by the nationalization, without any detailed rules as to the

(1) Cf. *Dep. St. Bul.*, vol., 15, (1946), p. 1004.
(2) Cf. *Dep. St. Bul.*, vol. 14, (1946), p. 761.

form of the compensation, its nature, amount, etc., also occur in a few cases in the form of the so called most favoured nation clauses.

As examples of this special form of treaty, which is frequently employed in limited spheres where it may be difficult to formulate future situations, the following agreements may be mentioned:

In connection with certain Swedish-Czech negotiations in Stockholm to fix the extent of the exchange of goods between the two countries, the Czech Minister in Stockholm sent the following Note to the Swedish Foreign Minister on 15th March, 1947:

> "I have the honour to inform your Excellency that concerning the application of the Czechoslovak Decrees Nos. 100, 101, 102, 103/1945 on nationalization, and regulations and measures regarding the introduction of state administration and confiscation, Swedish shareholders shall enjoy most favoured nation rights, particularly with respect to procedure, the basis for the calculation of compensation and the determination of the amount thereof".(1)

Similar most favoured nation clauses were laid down as between Norway and Poland,(2) between Sweden and Hungary,(3) and between Denmanrk and Poland in connection with the Danish-Polish trade negotiations in 1947.(4)

2. *Critical valuation.* The right assured in these latter treaties to the claimant country to be treated as most favoured nation in respect of procedure, basis of calculation and amount of compensation, has given no results in practice. The states bound by the treaties with some reason may insist that conditions in the individual case differ from those of the cases referred to by the claimants as the basis for most favoured nation treatment. The problems involved by the compensation claims will be so complicated, and the questions concerning the form of compensation, basis of its calculation, and its amount, will be bound up with future contra payments to such an extent that a direct comparison between different forms of settlement of compensation cannot be made.(5) But even where the most

(1) Cf. *S. Ö.*, 1947, p. 572.

(2) 4th February, 1946, cf. *Stortings proposition*, (1955), No. 103.

(3) 26th July, 1946, cf. *S. Ö.*, 1951, p. 145.

(4) The Agreement was not published, but was discussed inter alia in the newspaper *Politiken* for 14th May, 1949. The Agreement was dated 5th December, 1947.

(5) On the other hand most favoured nation clauses in connection with concrete definite agreements concerning the form of compensation can be

favoured nation clause is not employed, the agreements referred to here has proved ineffective, since, e. g., no American citizens have up till now succeded in getting compensation from Poland or Czechoslovakia.

It must consequently be admitted that the general liability to pay compensation assumed by the nationalizing state is not suited to solve the problems of compensation. The use of these agreements must be due to political expediency. The time when and the situation under which these agreements came into being point to the explanation that the agreements must be regarded exclusively as showing an accommodating attitude on the part of the nationalizing state in respect of claims for compensation from nationals in a country with which it is desired to establish trade relations, etc., at a time when the nationalizing state is not prepared to conclude concrete agreements on the payment of compensation.

It has also been shown that compensation agreements in general terms have been regarded by the states as provisional and have therefore been superseded — or attempts have been made to have them superseded — by one of the other forms of compensation agreements.(1)

---

of great significance, cf. the agreement concluded between Belgium and France on 18th February, 1949 concerning compensation to the shareholders in the nationalized French gas and electrical power industry. Here the actual object of the compensation and the method of valuation was laid down in detail in the French legislation, and the points to determine who can be considered as most favoured are enumerated in § 2 of the Agreement where is is stated: "In particular if at any future date the French Government grants to another country, for the benefit of the nationals thereof, payments by way of compensation for similar stock of sums of a greater amount, or yielding higher interest, or payable in a smaller number of annual instalments or enjoying certain transfer facilities, the Belgian Government shall be entitled to claim, on behalf of its nationals, the substitution of the compensation conditions accorded to the nationals of such other country for the procedure laid down in the present agreement". (*U. N. Treaty Series*, vol. 31, p. 175).

Cf. also Swedish-Polish treaty of 28th February, 1947, art. 11, (*S. Ö.*, 1947, p. 131) and the Danish-Polish treaty of 12th May, 1949, art. 9 (*Lovtidende* C, (1949), p. 571), which also contain a most favoured nation clause.

(1) Cf. the Survey of Forms of Compensation in Appendix B.

B. *Agreements providing for direct individual compensation.*

1. *Practice.* Agreements concerning direct individual compensation occur when the states implicated, in addition to agreeing — or confirming — the liability of the nationalizing state to pay compensation, lay down certain rules of procedure and possible facilities in connection with the rules laid down in the nationalization laws, whereupon it is left to the individual foreign physical or juridical person to put in his claim and provide documentary evidence directly to the authorities of the state liable to pay compensation. The compensation then, to the extent that the claim is admitted, will be paid direct to the party entitled to receive compensation.

This system was used in the treaties concluded soon after the end of the Second World War in respect of compensation for nationalized property.

In the agreement entered into by Switzerland and Czechoslovakia on 18th December, 1946, e. g., it is left entirely to the individual to enforce his claim for compensation. With regard to the facillities which the compensating state should accord to the foreigner, it is stated in art. 6 inter alia:

> "... zu diesem zwecke geniessen die schweizerischen Interessenten alle in den einschlägigen tschechoslowakischen Gesetzen und Verordnungen vorgesehenen Rechte und Vorteile. Tschechoslowakischer seits wird ihnen unter allen Umständen die Möglichkeit eingeräumt, die zur Einreichung ihrer Begehren und Vorschläge bei der tschechoslowakischen Behörden nötigen Mittel zu verwenden. Dies gilt insbesondere für Besichtigungen der Unternehmungen an Ort und Stelle ... für die Fühlungnahme mit dem leitenden Personal, die Überprüfung von Bilanzen, technischen und finanziellen Berichten von Geschäftsbüchern u. s. w. sowie auch für die Anfertigung von Kopien der erwähnten Schriftstücke und Dokumente ..."(1)

An example of an agreement providing for direct individual compensation, but where the home state of the party entitled to compensation is in somewhat closer contact with the nationalizing state, is to be found in the compensation treaty concluded by an exchange of Notes on 24th January, 1948 between Great Britain and Poland. In art. 12 it is laid down that compensation shall be payable to certain British owners of and shareholders in nationalized undertakings, and that the compensation will be paid direct to those entitled.

(1) Quoted according to Bindschedler, *op. cit.*, p. 73.

The individual concerned must raise his claim himself, but in art. 22 Poland pledged herself to grant to the said British citizens all necessary support and facilities to enable them to do this. These facilities are defined in the treaty as follows:

"art. 22 b: . . . the right —
(i) to visit nationalized undertakings;
(ii) to obtain such information regarding the condition and value of nationalized undertakings as may reasonably be required for the presentation and prosecution of claims to compensation; and
(iii) to participate in preparing detailed inventories of the element of property of nationalized undertakings and to submit comments and explanations on the relevant protocols of delivery and receipt . . ."(1)

At the same time, however, a mixed Anglo-Polish commission was set up, not with the task of deciding the merits of the individual British claims, but to watch the implementing of the agreement and to make recommendations to the governments concerning necessary alterations, if any, and at the express request of the governments in individual instances to decide disputes between the private claimant and the Polish state, and in other ways interpret the agreement of the two states, cf. Appendix B of the treaty.

A similar arrangement was made in connection with the Swedish-Polish agreement of 28th February, 1947(2), where Poland (art. 2) undertook to pay appropriate compensation direct to Swedish nationals in consequence of the nationalization. Only in the event of failure of the negotiations between the Polish authorities and the Swedish shareholders the mixed Swedish-Polish commission, set up in accordance with art. 6 of the treaty, was to intervene. It was also the task of the commission in this case to interpret the compensation agreement on behalf of the two governments.

By an exchange of Notes dated 19th March, 1947,(3) Belgium came to an arrangement with Czechoslovakia to the effect that Belgian shareholders in nationalized undertakings should receive compensation in case these shareholders had made good their claims in conformity with the Czech national regulations. To simplify the procedure — which was that direct individual compensation should be paid — it was, however, agreed that a Belgian authority should

(1) The whole text of the treaty can be found in *The International Law Quarterly*, vol. 2, (1948), p. 544.

(2) Cf. *S. Ö.*, 1947, p. 131.

(3) *U.N. Treaty Series*, 23 p. 37.

collect the necessary documents and forward them to the Czech Ministry of Finance, cf. art. 1.

Based on similar principles was the arrangement agreed upon between Belgium and France by a treaty of 18th February, 1949, with subsequent amendments,(1) for the purpose of obtaining compensation for Belgian interests in the nationalized gas and electric power industry; it was laid down in art. 4 that the Belgian shareholders should apply with their share certificates to La Caisse nationale de l'Energie in Paris, where the shares would then be exchanged for Government Bonds in accordance with the compensation conditions agreed upon between the two governments. In this case, too, it was left to the individual to prove that in respect of nationality and method of acquisition he complied with the conditions for receiving compensation laid down in the treaty. Until 31st December, 1949, however, a Belgian office existed where the Belgian nationals could apply with the necessary documentation.

This form of compensation, described here as direct individual compensation, is also provided for in agreements between France and Czechoslovakia, dated 6th August, 1948(2), Holland and Czechoslovakia, dated 4th November, 1949, Switzerland and France under the date of 21st November, 1949,(3) and between Great Britain and France, dated 11th April, 1951.(4)

2. *Critical valuation.* These agreements on direct individual compensation, where the initiative and the trouble of enforcing the claim for compensation is left to the private individuals who feel themselves affected by nationalization, seem attractive. The individual claimant, before he raises his claim for compensation, must decide whether the trouble and expense involved bear a reasonable proportion to the nature and amount of the claim, and this probably results in a number of doubtful or minor claims being abandoned.(5) This arrangement avoids the individual compensation claims being placed on the international plane, where other and irrelevant considerations might exert an influence.(6)

(1) Cf. *U. N. Treaty Series*, vol. 31, p. 173 and vol. 73, p. 257.

(2) Cf. *Journal officiel*, 11th November, 1951.

(3) *Amtl. Samml.*, (1950), p. 21.

(4) *T. S.*, s. 34, and 35, (1951).

(5) Bindschedler, *op. cit.*, p. 74 and Odevall, "Globalersättning för ekonomiska intressen i utlandet", *N. T. I. R.*, vol. 24, (1954), p. 20, both agree that these agreements fit in with the Western individualistic legal view.

(6) But cf. the exchange of Notes mentioned above p. 82 between the Swedish and Polish governments on 18th March, 1947.

But this form of compensation agreement presupposes that the country of the national entitled to compensation is justified in its confidence that its nationals will receive fair treatment, and that the state liable to pay the compensation is really willing to and capable of fulfilling its obligations in accordance with the agreements it has entered into.

But apart from the agreements concluded with France these elements have been absent in actual fact. The private claimant, whether a person or a company, normally has not been able to enforce his claims, and in the few cases where in pursuance of these agreements compensation has been paid, the amount of compensation has apparently been determined by the question whether the nationalizing state has been interested in future co-operation with the private claimant(1) — possible in different fields.

There are also to be taken into account the economic-political difficulties and misgivings on the part of the states both in the case of direct and indirect individual compensation, which problem will be discussed below under chapter C.

As the difficulties inherent in this form of compensation settlement, have proved overwhelming in most cases most of the agreements of this kind have been superseded by other forms.

C. *Agreements providing for indirect individual compensation.*

1. *Practice.* This form of compensation occurs in those cases where the physical or juridical person affected by the nationalization has to present his claim for compensation to the nationalizing state through his government. The question of the recognition of the claim and its amount is settled in each individual case by negotiation between the governments involved, and similarly the compensation is paid to the claimant's government. These negotiations may take place either through the ordinary diplomatic channels, or through the setting up of a mixed commission to determine the individual claims.

(1) Thus it is stated in *Kunglig Majestäts Proposition* of 3rd March, 1950, that certain large Swedish undertakings, in connection with an agreement concerning fresh deliveries to Poland, in pursuance of the treaty of 28th February, 1947, "shall be ensured good prospects of receiving compensation for compulsory measures of different kinds, and agreements on this basis will be arranged." It is, however, added that a general regulation of the Swedish compensation claims does not appear to be within reach. *Riksdagens Protokoll*, vol. 16 (1950) prp. No. 187, p. 11.

After negotiations had been going on for a number of years between the Mexican Government and the Government of Great Britain on its own behalf and on behalf of the Dutch Government, in connection with the Mexican nationalization of the oil fields, etc., agreements were entered into between Mexico and these two states on 7th February, 1947, concerning the procedure to determine the amounts of the compensation which Mexico undertook to pay.(1) In these agreements it was decided to appoint experts who were to produce a report within a given time, giving an estimated valuation of the nationalized property. Art. 17 of the treaty with Holland goes on to say(2):

> "Within a month of the receipt of the report ... of the experts, the two Governments shall initiate diplomatic negotiations with a view to fix ... the sum to be paid ... to those Netherlands subjects who, by such methods as the two Governments may determine, prove their participation as shareholders, at the time of publication of this note, in the properties referred to."

It is noticeable that Holland was to have the compensation paid by Great Britain as and when Mexico paid, it obviously being due to the influence of Britain that Holland obtained compensation.

An agreement concerning indirect individual compensation was similarly concluded between Denmark and Poland by the Protocol signed in Warsaw 12th May, 1949, regarding Danish interests and property.(3) The provisions of art. 7 contain regulations to the effect that the notification of rights and interests in nationalized undertakings can be made to the registry of property surrendered and taken over set up in accordance with Polish legislation. The notification may be made either direct by the interested parties or through the Danish Legation in Warsaw. Art. 10 at the same time provides that there should be appointed a mixed Danish-Polish commission whose task is laid down thus:

> "(The commission's task is to) ... achieve a solution in each individual case, to discuss any problems that may arise in connection with the fixing of amounts of compensations due to Danish claimants, as well as problems otherwise affecting Danish interests and property in Poland ..."

(1) The agreement with Holland will be found in *U.N. Treaty Series*, vol. 3, p. 13. The agreement with Great Britain will be found in *U.N. Treaty Series*, vol. 6, p. 55. A similar agreement was also concluded between the United States and Mexico, 29th September, 1943, cf. *Dep. St. Bul*, (1943), p. 230.

(2) The same provision is found in the treaty concluded with Great Britain, Art. 17.

(3) Cf. *Lovtidende* C, (1949), p. 567.

It is further laid down that in the event that the Danish Government should not consider the compensation fixed adequate, the matter should be discussed between the governments of the two countries (art. 11, para. 3). If a solution still proved unobtainable by this means, the matter should go to arbitration. Lastly, it was agreed that negotiations concerning the payment of the compensation and its transfer to Denmark should be entered upon in the middle of 1950.

Similar agreements were concluded between the United States and Poland, 27th December, 1947, between Italy and Jugoslavia, 23rd May, 1949 and between Turkey and Jugoslavia, 5th January, 1950.

2. *Critical valuation.* The payment of compensation in the form described here as indirect individual compensation, is in close conformity with the traditional diplomatic handling of the claims of private citizens or companies against foreign states. By virtue of the position and influence of the state entitled to compensation, this form of agreement often should have a good chance of achieving the desired result.

The existing international treaty practice, however, shows that this form of individual compensation after all is not particularly attractive either to any of the parties. The nationalizing state in fixing the compensation for a given property will be inclined to try keeping the value to be fixed as low as possible, out of consideration for the example the decission may set with a view to claims that may later be raised. From corresponding motives the state representing the claimant will be disinclined to accept a valuation which is perhaps reasonable in the given case. Negotiations on such a basis are apt to end in a deadlock.

Apart from the cases where the nature and extent of all compensation claims are known to both parties when the negotiations begin — cf. the art. 17 quoted above of the treaty between Mexico and Great Britain and Holland, where negotiations concerning the amount of the compensation were not to begin until after the experts' valuation of the property concerned had been received — payment of indirect individual compensation has proved unworkable in practice, and the states have had these agreements, too, superseded by treaties providing for the payment of global compensation.

D. *Agreements providing for global compensation.*

1. *Practice.* Global compensation means that in settlement of a number of claims arising out of homogeneous circumstances, the state that is pledged to render compensation pays a lump-sum accepted by the claimant state, both on behalf of its nationals and on its own behalf, so that no further claims derived from the action that gave rise to the compensationclaim can be raised, either by the states concerned, or by there nationals with their consent.

This form of compensation payment, whose characteristic feature is to be found rather in the »balance receipt« given against payment covering a number of known and unknown claims, than in the estimate of the amount of the compensation, has often, as Whiteman shows,(1) been used in international practice. Whiteman thus enumerates 36 cases in the period 1802—1934, in which global arrangements have been preferred by states. Denmark, e. g., formerly in 28th March, 1830, made a global agreement. By a convention with the United States of the said date concerning the "Settlement of the claims of American Nationals for compensation in respect of Seizure and Forfeiting of Ships and Cargoes" Denmark promised to pay kr. 650,000 in compensation to the United States, art. 1.(2) This amount was to be paid in three instalments, art. 2, whereupon the United States Government, on its own behalf and on behalf of American nationals, declared itself satisfied in respect of every claim in connection with the military events that led to the seizure and forfeiture of the American ships.

Global compensation agreements have proved immensely practicable in the settlement of claims for compensation resulting from measures of nationalization. The earlist of this group of agreements were concluded between Sweden and Soviet Russia, 30th May, 1941, and between Sweden and Jugoslavia, 12th April, 1947,(3) and as can be seen from the "Survey of Forms of Compensation", attached *infra*

(1) *Damages in International Law*, vol. III, (1932), p. 2068. Cf. also Bindschedler, *op. cit.*, p. 80 and Odevall, *op. cit.*, p. 17.

(2) Whiteman, *loc. cit.*, p. 2068 k, no. 6, cf. Odevall, *op. cit.*, p. 18, who states that the compensation shall be paid in "Spanish ring-stamped dollars". This term is not used in the original text of the treaty, which is to be found in *Danske Tractater efter 1800*, first collection, vol. I, (1872), p. 139 ff.

(3) These agreements have not been published, as they are regarded as confidential by the Swedish government. From *Kunglig Majestäts prp.* no. 350, (1946), p. 22 and no. 187, (1950), p. 15, it appears, however, that in both cases it is a question of agreements concerning global compensation, cf. also no. 310, (1947), p. 25.

as Appendix B, by far the great majority of recent compensation agreements have provided for global compensation, just as most of the agreements concerning other forms of compensation have been superseded by treaties involving global arrangements.

2. *Critical valuation.* The expediency of this form of compensation, despite the fact that the compensation seldom amounts to 100 % of the sum claimed, is to be found in the following circumstances. First, the fixing of the amount of compensation at an approximate amount of the sum claimed is less complicated for all parties. Secondly, because of the simpler procedure, the amount of the compensation can be decided relatively quickly, which is nearly always an advantage to the claimants. Thirdly, the problem of individual doubtful claims can be solved by regulating the lump-sum compensation upward or downward, without the legal problems involved by the doubtful claims needing to be investigated in detail and perhaps cause conflict as between the two parties.(1) Fourthly, both contracting states know that all claims for compensation due to nationalization are now finally settled, so that further negotiation, involving expense and political irritation, will be avoided. Fifthly, exchangeproblems and questions of future contra payments, if any, on the part of the state to whom compensation is due, all will be settled far more easily when the amount of the compensation is finally fixed in a lump-sum agreement.

3. *A problem of validity.* Whereas the agreements concluded in respect of global compensation broadly speaking are juridically identical with regard to the obligation to pay and principles governing the fixing of the amount of the compensation, there is, as stated by

(1) Among the Danish claims for compensation in connection with nationalizations in Poland, there was one that was based on the acquisition of real property by a Danish national by means of a contingent conveyance concluded before 1st September, 1939, but in such a way that the condition making the conveyance absolute not being fulfilled until 6th September, 1939. Since in accordance with the Danish-Polish Protocol of 12th May, 1949, art. 4, the Polish state was only bound to pay compensation to persons who, before 1st September 1939, had become owners of property that was subsequently nationalized, the Polish representatives at the negotiations maintained (in conformiy with lex rei sitae, i. e., in casu German law) that the acquisition of the property was not complete until the condition was fulfilled. In Danish law, however, it is held that the subject-matter of the contract passes when the contract, as the case may be, the contingent contract, is concluded. — In connection with the agreement in respect of global compensation Poland agreed to pay an equitable compensation for this property.

Odevall, a peculiar feature connected with the formulation of some of these agreements in so far as regards the provisions to the effect that all problems of compensation shall be definitively settled by the compensation agreement in question.

As examples of the formulation of these agreements reference can be made to the Danish-Polish Protocol of 26th February, 1953,(1) which in art. 2 contains the following provision:

> "On completion of the payment of the sum of 5,700,00 Danish Kroner, the Danish Government will consider all the Danish claims, enumerated in art. 1,(2) as definitively settled. This settlement has the effect of discharging the Polish government, in respect of Danish interested parties and their claims, from all liability."

This provision involves that no Danish national will be able to bring any further claims against the Polish government.

In the Anglo-Jugoslav agreement of 23rd December, 1948(3) a similar quitclaim is contained in art. II, which states that the global sum will be received:

> "... in full satisfaction and discharge of all claims of British nationals arising on or before the date of signature of the present Agreement out of various Jugoslav measures affecting British property."

And it is added in the next paragraph of the article that the United Kingdom

> "... on their own behalf and on behalf of British nationals shall release the Government of Jugoslavia from all liability, including liability for payment to British nationals, in respect of the claims mentioned ..."

In contrast to these formulations which contain an express quitclaim in respect of further claims for compensation, the global compensation agreements concluded, for instance, by Sweden and Norway, contain no such quitclaim restraining their nationals from raising such claims later against the government which is paying compensation.

In the agreement between Sweden and Poland of 16th November, 1949(4) it is laid down in art. 2 that the Swedish government guar-

---

(1) *Lovtidende C*, (1954), p. 1.

(2) Art. 1 covers inter alia: "all Danish property, rights, ad interests which are affected by the Polish legislation ... or by any other measure taken by the Polish state or by its organs".

(3) *T. S.*, No. 2, (1949).

(4) *S. Ö.*, 1950, p. 921.

antees that the Polish government after payment of the lump-sum compensation shall not pay any further claims in respect of the nationalization of Swedish property, and further, that the Swedish government guarantees — from the time when the agreement comes into force and as long as the provisions are fulfilled — that it will not give support to claims for compensation on the part of Swedish claimants.

The agreement between Sweden and Hungary(1) of 31st March, 1951, includes a similar provision, but the Swedish guarantee is more closely defined and it is laid down in art. 3 that if Swedish claims for compensation:

> "... nevertheless should be carried into legal effect, the Hungarian government is entitled to deduct as against the Swedish government any losses suffered by Hungary in respect thereof..."

The agreement concluded 23rd December, 1955, between Norway and Poland, contains in art. 3 the following provision:

> "The Norwegian government declares besides that after the conclusion of this agreement and after the Polish government has fulfilled its provisions, the Norwegian government will neither on its own behalf nor on behalf of its nationals bring against the Polish government any claims which have arisen before the signing of this agreement and which originate from Polish measures of nationalization or expropriation or from other similar measures, nor will it give any support to such claims."(2)

It appears to be clearly implied in the case of these formulations that unsettled claims will not lapse by the concluding and fulfilment of agreements providing for global compensation. The promise by the state receiving compensation not to support future private claims — particularly in connection with a guarantee as the one given by the Swedish government — means, however, that the nationalizing states also when concluding agreements formulated as mentioned above can be sure that their measures of nationalization will not involve further economic obligations than follows from the global compensation agreement.

Since the practice followed by Sweden and Norway cannot thus be based on economic views or considerations of international policy, the question arises whether this practice is dictated by legal considerations. This might be the case if according to its national law the Swedish or Norwegian government was not entitled to renounce the rights of its nationals as against other states, and if

(1) *S. Ö.*, 1951, p. 146.

(2) *Stortingets prp.*, no. 103, (1955), p. 5.

such transgression of its national competency would possibly render the treaty invalid in international law.

It must however be assumed that the power of a state in international law to make arrangements concerning the affairs of its nationals in relation to other states is unlimited. A state must have a free hand in international negotiations concerning the affairs of its nationals and thus must be able to regulate their status as against a foreign state under proper consideration of existing political conditions. This must hold good, even if a government thereby exceeds its national constitutional competency in respect of its citizens and even if this was known to the other party to the agreement, since this is the only way in which there can be confidence in international negotiation. It may very well be — particularly in the case of the compensation agreements under discussion — that a government deliberately and openly sets aside the interests of an individual — and perhaps cranky — citizen in order to arrive at a settlement that benefits the majority of those entitled to compensation. In that case it would be wholly unreasonable and in the interests of none of the contracting states that, for fear of the possible invalidity of such an agreement in international law, the state undertaken to pay compensation should feel impelled to investigate and examine the motives of the other state behind such course of action. The party in question must be entitled to assume that the relationship between a state and its nationals is a matter of national law with which the international legal agreement is not concerned at all.

Since a global agreement will thus be valid in international law, even if the state receiving compensation possibly transgresses its constitutional competency, the Swedish and Norwegian practice must be dictated solely by considerations of national law, such as, for example, the fear that the government might be liable in damages if without legal basis it renounces the rights of its nationals as against other states. This problem falls outside the scope of this work and will not be pursued further. It should only be mentioned that in Danish law there is scarcely authority for the government to renounce the compensation claims of its nationals against other states. Although it will not be illegal for Danish authorities not to protect Danish interests in foreign countries it cannot be concluded therefrom that the Danish government should be entitled definitively on behalf of its nationals to renounce their rights. It will, however, not be easy in practice to prove that by a global agreement the Danish government should have imposed upon a citizen an economic loss, which is the pre-condition for the liability of the government to pay damages to materialize.

§ 16.

FOR WHAT PROPERTY IS COMPENSATION GIVEN?

A. *Proprietary rights.*

The compensation agreements that have been concluded in their formulation are particularly comprehensive with regard to the subject matter of compensation.

The Danish-Polish agreement of 12th May, 1949, thus speaks in general terms of "interests and property", and the agreement of 26th February, 1953, as objects of compensation enumerates, "property, rights, and interests". Similar wording is used in the British treaties, for example, in the agreement with Jugoslavia of 23rd December, 1948, and with Czechoslovakia of 28th September, 1949, which use the terms "property, rights, and interests". The Norwegian agreement with Bulgaria of 2nd December, 1955 refers to "interests", while in the agreement with Poland of 23rd December, 1955, the word "assets" is used. The Swedish agreements also use the comprehensive term"interests", such as, for example, the agreement with Poland of 28th February, 1947, and likewise the Franco-Polish agreement of 19th March, 1948. More instructive, however, is the agreement concluded between Switzerland and Czechoslovakia on 18th December, 1946, which covers "propriété, participations, créances et propriété intellectuelle, telle que brevets, licences, procédés de fabrication, plans, marque de fabrique et raison sociales". All the treaties also provide that compensation is to be paid for shares in the aforesaid rights and interests.

It appears that the subject matter of compensation is nationalized property in the widest sense, i. e. comprising every kind of property of economic value.

It must especially be noted that the goodwill of an activity, in the sense of the capitalized value of future profit, is to a certain extent included. As will be shown *infra* in § 18, the compensation for nationalized property is in principle fixed on the basis of the market value of the property at the time of nationalization, and expectations in respect of future profit is a factor which can influence the determination of this amount. This view is particularly clear when, as for example in France, compensation is paid to foreign shareholders in nationalized companies, calculated on the basis of the value of the shares as quoted on the stock exchange at a given time, as the stock exchange price is determined with a view to expected future earnings, cf. *supra* § 12 and the treaties between

Belgium and France of 18th February, 1949, and between Great Britain and France of 11th April, 1951. The determination, however, of the final market value is influenced by so comprehensive discretionary elements that the question of goodwill under discussion here will fundamentally be of little practical significance for the calculation of the compensation.

B. *Creditors' Claims.*

Nationalization of an activity normally comprises all the assets and liabilities of the business. This raises the question of the position of creditors of nationalized activities with regard to compensation.

This question in practice is settled in various ways.

In the agreement between Denmark and Poland of 12th May, 1949, it is thus understood, art. 3, that claims against nationalized activities shall be raised against the former owners, and this will be considered when the lawful compensation to be paid to these owners is determined.(1)

This arrangement appears to be extremely unpractical, for it presupposes that Poland pays compensation to its own nationals, and it cannot be in the interest of Poland that other states should have to interfere in case the Polish debtor refuses payment on the plea that he has received no compensation from the Polish state with which to meet his obligations. This arrangement also involves the unreasonable — and unjustifiable — risk for the creditor that the recipient of the compensation may be unwilling to pay the debt, originating in the nationalized activity, an attitude which may cause considerable trouble in international relations, or further the debtor may become insolvent before the claim can be enforced.

This form of arrangement actually in general has been abandoned by the states, and global agreements concluded now all contain provisions to the effect that the claims of creditors form part of the lump-sum. In the Danish-Polish treaty of 26th February, 1953, it is e. g., laid down that the Polish government shall pay compensation to the Danish government for inter alia:

> "3. Danish claims, including bonds, against debtors in Poland whose property is affected by the Polish legislation or by those measures taken in pursuance thereof".(2)

(1) A similar arrangement is provided for in the Anglo-Polish agreement of 24th January, 1948, art. 15, taken together with art. 16 in fine.

(2) The same wording is used in the Swedish-Polish treaty of 16th January, 1949.

This provision, however, has been given an unreasonably wide wording, and ought to be so understand as to cover only claims in respect of nationalized property.

Lastly, it should be mentioned that the majority of nationalization laws give creditors a less favourable legal position than that accorded to holders of proprietary claims. The Czech Decree no. 100/45 §5, para. 2 thus annuls claims that are based upon "economical unjustified debts".(1) In Poland only certain obligations are kept alive.(2) By the law of 11th May, 1948, art. 14, the Roumanian state annulled all claims due to bad administration, and in Hungary all claims that solely benefited owners and shareholders were likewise annulled in pursuance of the nationalization law of 1948, art. 9.

These national provisions, however, must in principle be regarded as having no effect as regards claims to compensation in international law. In considering them from the angle of international law the only relevant consideration is whether the creditor's claim was acquired in conformity with the national rules in force at the time of acquisition. Whether the views quoted in the laws in actual fact have influenced the fixing of the amounts of compensation cannot, however, be established without a close investigation of the individual claims raised in the various government negotiations.

§ 17.

WHO CAN RAISE A CLAIM FOR COMPENSATION?

The rules of international law concerning compensation for nationalization only apply to foreign property. International law does not regulate the relations between a state and its own nationals, and if the nationalizing state therefore should have a liability in international law to pay compensation to another state or its nationals, the property in question must have a certain national connection with the claimant state.

This pre-condition for the application of the rules of international law raises the following questions:

A. *What is it that decides the national character of the property?*

1. *The property has no independent nationality.* If the property in question does not possess an independent nationality, the ques-

(1) Cf. Doman, *op. cit.*, p. 1158.

(2) Cf. above p. 47 and p. 66 concerning the nationalization law of 3rd January, 1946, art. 6.

tion depends on the nationality of the party to whom the property belongs. If the owner is Danish, the property will as a result be considered Danish, even if it is situated in a foreign country. Such property will thus be subject to the rules of international law.

There can scarcely be any doubt about this.

2. *The property has independent nationality.* It is different, on the other hand, if the property, whose national character is to be determined, possesses, under the national legislation, an independent nationality differing from the nationality of the party to whom it belongs.

This situation may exist where the object of natianalization is a so called juridical person, for example, a company of shareholders, for it may often be that a company has an independent nationality. The question then arises as to whether the national character of an activity in the form of a company etc. is to be determined by the nationality of the juridical person or by the nationality of the person to whom the company belongs.

The problem is not merely academic. A Danish national, for example, is the majority shareholder in a company which has its *situs* in Poland and is registered in Poland, just as the business of the whole company is carried on in Poland. In Danish law the company cannot be considered to be Danish.(1) In Polish law the company will be regarded as Polish. The problem then is whether, under reference to the Polish character of the company, Poland can nationalize the said company without the risk of Danish interference, on the plea that the nationalization of such a company is outside the sphere regulated by international law.

It seems that the problem must be so solved that the Polish state, to the extent to which foreign interests are implicated, must observe the rules of international law as they exist in this field. The rules of international law concerning the protection of foreign property aim at safeguarding the interests of foreign states and their nationals; and the interests a foreign national has in a company, in his capacity as shareholder, must in general be regarded as a right to a share in the property of the company proportionate to the amount of the shares held. The person in question is the owner of this share in the same way as he is the owner of a thing or a claim, and when the value of such share is extinquished by the nationalization of the company, there is the same need for the international legal rules

(1) Cf. Krenchel, *Håndbog i dansk Aktieret*, (1954), p. 44.

to protect this form of property as in case of real property or chattels. Company law normally is not against this result, since in consequence of the nationalization the company is actually dissolved, and the shareholder's right therefore manifests itself as an immediate right to a share in the company's property. Further, the fact that the nationalizing states in some cases have preserved the company form after the transfer of the activity to state ownership seems to lead to no other result. Since it must be stressed that even though the fact that a company has a certain independent nationality can be practicable and reasonable in relation to the national legislation of a country, this nationality ought not to influence the question whether the juridical person enjoys protection under the international law of aliens vis-á-vis the state whose nationality — on motives that are quite different and have nothing to do with international law — is assigned to the juridical person.

This problem should be decided on the basis of true ownership alone.(1)(2)

This view is also recognized in international legal practice, as in the case *Delagoa Bay and East African Railway Company,* where both Great Britain and the United States presented claims for compensation in consequence of the annulment by Portugal of a concession belonging to a Portuguese company. The shares were on British and American hands. In the submission for arbitration Portugal recognized the foreign character of this company.(3)

The view advocated, i. e., that true ownership alone is decisive, also as regards juridical persons, is confirmed, too, by the compensation negotiations conducted between Switzerland and Czechoslovakia. In the treaty concluded between these two states on 18th December, 1946, it is laid down that compensation is to be paid for nationalized Swiss companies, i. e. companies in which the Swiss capital amounts to more than 50 %. In the supplementary protocol dated 7th February, 1947(4) an addition is made to this provision:

---

(1) Cf. also Jones, "Claims on behalf of Nationals who are Shareholders in Foreign Companies", *B. Y. I. L.*, vol. 26, (1949), p. 225—258, who after going through international practice seems to come to the same conclusion.

(2) On the procedural question as to what criteria are decisive of the competency of a state to exercise international protection of a juridical person, see *infra* under B.

(3) Cf. in addition Hyde, *International Law,* vol. 2 (1945) p. 904—906, and Hackworth, *op. cit.*, vol. V., (1941), p. 841 ff. and the examples given there.

(4) *Recueil officiel,* (1948), p. 556.

"D'une façon générale, il est bien entendu que, d'autre part, les participations minoritaires suisses bénéficient également de cette protection ..."

It may further be mentioned that it appears from the list published in "Journal Officiel" for 11th November, 1951, naming the interests for which compensation was paid in pursuance of the compensation agreement concluded between France and Poland, 19th March, 1948, that compensation was paid for French interests in 54 companies, 47 of which were Polish companies according to Polish law. In 7 of these Polish companies the French interests were minority interests, amounting to between 11—31% of the share capital.

In those cases where this problem has not been specifically dealt with in the compensation agreements it must consequently be assumed that the treaty must be interpreted on the lines stated above.

B. *To whom must the property belong?*

1. *Physical persons.* Practically speaking it is a uniform rule in the treaties of compensation that the property for which compensation is to be paid shall belong to persons who are nationals of that state which presents the claim for compensation. That nationality is decisive for diplomatic protection is generally recognized in the theory(1) and practice of international law.

The problem of what persons a state can regard as its nationals is solved in international law by a reference to the national legal systems,(2) which are free in this respect, provided the person in question has a connection of a certain quality with the state, and that the state does not abuse its competence to grant status of nationality with a view to evading the regulations of the international law of aliens.

With regard to physical persons the establishment of the nationality of a given person presents no difficulty in practice, since nationality is a criterion that can be objectively ascertained.

In the special case where a person has double nationality, the general rules of international law on this point must apply, i. e. that

(1) Cf. for example, Borchard, *op. cit.*, p. 15: "... nationality is the most important factor, for it is by virtue of the bond of nationality that (the alien) is entitled to invoke the aid of a specific protector and that a definitive member of the international society of states has the right to interpose in his behalf to secure a guarantee for his rights and reparation for their violation."

(2) Cf. the *Hague Convention* of 12th April, 1930, art. 1: "It is for each state by its legislation to decide who are its nationals ..."

a claim for compensation for nationalized property belonging to such a person, cannot be presented against a state which also — lawfully — claims the person in question as one of its nationals. The nationalizing state moreover may choose as competent protector the state with which the person with double nationality has the greatest bond.(1)

It might be asked whether a person's domicile in a state ought not to be sufficient to make this state his competent protector in international law, at any rate in those cases where the person in question possesses no nationality. It may indeed seem unreasonable that a stateless person, who, by his business activity in a given country, has acquired a claim against a nationalizing state, should have no opportunity of raising his claim through the authorities of the country which, for example, through taxation etc. receives a share of the proceeds of his activity. This seems the more unreasonable in view of the very long period that under the national legislations has to pass before an application for naturalisation can be entertained.

Existing international law(2) — as well as the compensation treaties, however, are unanimous on this point,(3) insisting unconditionally on nationality in order that a person affected by nationalization may claim through the government in question.

2. *Juridical persons.* The nationality of juridical persons however has given rise to a certain amount of doubt.(4) Nor in this field is

---

(1) Cf. The *Hague Convention* of 12th April, 1930, art. 4 and 5, and also the case of *Baron Frederic de Born v. Jugoslavia* (1926), Ross & Foighel, *Studiebog*, p. 207.

(2) Cf. however, the case of *Martin Koszta* (1853), *Moore, Digest*, III, § 490, where the United States considered itself to be the competent protector of a person who was domiciled in the United States and was for the time being living in Turkey. The case has been strongly criticized, and has been justified on the grounds of the very special circumstances surrounding it, including the fact that Koszta had applied for American citizenship. Borchard, *op. cit.*, p. 570—574.

(3) Cf. however, Wehberg, who, in *Annuaire*, vol. 43 I, (1950), p. 110, states that a private agreement was concluded between Switzerland and Poland, whereby Poland undertook to pay compensation for property belonging to stateless persons who are domiciled in or who own property situated in Switzerland.

(4) Cf. Borum, *Lovkonflikter*, (1948), p. 108—109, and in greater detail Louis-Lucas: "Remarques relatives à la détermination de la nationalité des sociétés", *La semaine juridique*, (1953), p. 1104, and Mann, "Zum Problem der Staatsangehörigkeit der juristischen Person", *Festschrift für Martin Wolf*, (1952), p. 271 ff.

there any direct solution offered by international law, which refers to the national legal systems. Whether a juridical person, for example, a company of shareholders in respect of nationality can be regarded as belonging to state A must be decided solely in accordance with A's national laws.(1)

Just as in the case of the determination of the nationality of physical persons, the bonds of nationality laid down in the national laws as regards juridical persons vary from country to country. Frequently one of the following criteria are employed as the basis for the determination of nationality:

the situs of the company,
the registration of the company,
the nationality of persons controling the company.

The existing divergencies between the national laws has also found expression in the compensation treaties that have been concluded.

The Danish-Polish Protocol II of 26th January, 1953, for instance covers "... commercial undertakings which are located in Denmark", art. V. On the same lines is the Swedish-Polish Protocol of 16th November, 1949, which in art. 5 contains the following provision:

"As Swedish there shall be considered ... juridical persons or commercial undertakings situated in Sweden".

The treaties concluded by Great Britain are based upon a different criterion. In the treaties with Jugoslavia of 23rd December, 1948, with Czechoslovakia of 28th September, 1949, and with Poland of 24th January, 1948 and 11th November, 1954, it is thus uniformly stated:

"For the purpose of the present agreement, 'British Nationals' shall mean —

...

(ii) Companies, firms and associations incorporated or constituted under the laws in force in the territory of the United Kingdom of Great Britain and Northern Ireland, Canada, the Commonwealth etc. ..."

(1) § 2 of the Danish law No. 132 of 30th March, 1946, concerning the Confiscation of German and Japanese property, apparently lays down when a company is German. — The explanation of this is probably that a "German" company for the purpose of that law is identical with an enemy company and as regards this question Danish legislation must have a free hand. On the other hand, this determination of the nationality of companies can scarcely have any significance in other relations.

Although both "situs" and "registration" can be fitting characteristics for the determination of the status of a company in national law, for example, in relation to industrial and fiscal legislation, it does not appear reasonable that without taking into consideration the real economic interests underlying a given juridical person these criteria should alone be decisive for the international competence to claim protection. This was expressed very clearly by Borchard in l'Institut de droit international, at the meeting of the Institute in Cambridge in 1931, where Borchard supported the view that a company's situs, registration, etc. were not sufficient to establish this competence to claim protection.(1)

On the other hand it may be justly maintained that the determination of the international competence of a state to raise claims on the basis of the real economic interests can be extremely difficult, and in the same way there may be cases where an investigation of such interests cannot possibly be carried out.

In a number of compensation treaties weight has been attached to a combination of the different view.

The treaty concluded between Sweden and Hungary on 31st March, 1951, for instance, according to art. 2 covers: "... juridical persons or commercial concerns with their seat in Sweden or with preponderantly Swedish interests". Whereas it is still sufficient according to the Swedish view that a company is situated in Sweden, the formulation leaves open the possibility of considering also the real economic interest as the basis when determining whether a company is Swedish in this respect.

In its agreements Switzerland has attached importance to the interest in the company being Swiss, since, for example, the Swiss-Polish treaty of 25th June, 1949, covers juridical persons who have their "siège social en Suisse et comportant un intérêt suisse prépondérant". In its agreement with Poland of 19th March, 1948, France obtained compensation both for French companies and for companies under French control (art. 4 b and c). This treaty thus clearly implies that the national concept of company nationality is insufficient as a basis for claims for compensation.

---

(1) Cf. *Annuaire,* (1931) p. 297. On the subject of the juridical person Borchard further asserts: "The company is simply a form of organization, a veritable cloak, which allows individuals to enjoy their property, and an injury inflicted upon this form as such is pure fiction. It is the individuals who derive an advantage from the organization constituted in the form of a company and who are injured ..."

The United States also are of opinion that the real economic interest is decisive. In art. 2 of the agreement with Jugoslavia of 19th July, 1948, it is laid down that the agreement covers property which belongs to "corporations organized in the United States, provided that at least twenty per cent of a corporate claimant's outstanding securities of any class where owned directly or indirectly by American nationals."

In international compensation agreements consequently there is no uniform line, but as a matter of fact this is of no significance with regard to the rules of international law under discussion here, provided that the factors decisive for the nationality of a company, whose property is affected by measures of nationalization, all refer to the same country. However, if a juridical person has a national connection with two or more states, so that the company has a "double nationality", it must be presumed that the company's nationality in international law is determined with a view to the particular legal effect for which nationality is decisive. In deciding who is the competent protector in the case of the nationalization of the property of a juridical person, it must be presumed that the actual ownership, i. e., the real economic interests will be decesive. In the *Case concerning Certain German interests in Polish Upper Silesia,* the Permanent Court of International Justice pronounces as follows on the interpretation of the principle laid down in the Geneva Convention to the effect that the nationality of companies is determined by the nationality of the person who has the actual control of the company:(1)

> "The Geneva Convention does not ... define the factors which constitute control and the existence of which may involve the liquidation of a company's property. The Court is of opinion that the conception of control ... is an essentially economic one and that it contemplates a preponderant influence over the general policy. Criteria of an external nature, such as situation of the registered offices, the place of foundation, the legislation under which the Company has been formed, etc. which have long been applied without any relation to the question of liquidation, by the legislation and jurisprudence of the different countries, seem to have been replaced in the Geneva Convention, and in so far as concerns the liquidation régime, by a more elastic criterion which enables in spite of appearances, physical persons of a particular nationality to be reached ..."

It appears, however, from the description of the character of ownership usual in these treaties — see *infra* — that the states, who in

(1) *P. C. I. J. Series A.*, no. 7, p. 68—69.

their compensation treaties exclusively use a formal criterion such as situs, registration, etc., have no wish to abandon rights in companies which are outside their nationality according to these criteria but which with a view the real economic interest ought to be represented by the said state.

C. *What must be the character of national ownership?*

In the compensation agreements it is laid down that the property for which compensation is payable must belong to national physical or juridical persons, either directly or indirectly.

1. *Direct ownership.* Direct ownership hardly gives rise to any doubt, either in connection with individuals or companies.

2. *Indirect ownership.* Indirect ownership for the benefit of individuals or companies probably may only exist in case a person or a company is owner of a company (described in the following as companyII), which in its turn is the owner of property or interests affected by nationalization.

If company II is of the same nationality as the physical or juridical persons who own this company, compensation is payable already under the provision in the treaties to the effect that compensation is payable in respect of property directly belonging to national companies. The provision concerning indirect ownership consequently will be of importance only if company II has a nationality different from that of its owners.

Understood in this sense the frequently employed rule concerning indirect ownership appears to lead to unreasonable consequences:

> Ex. 1: A Danish citizen owns a number of shares in a German company (company II), which owns property in Poland. The property is nationalized and the German company suffers loss thereby.

The rule concerning indirect ownership appears to lead to the result that the Danish citizen, through his government, shall be able to raise claim for compensation corresponding to the proportion of his share in the total assets of the company. It seems that this result must be rejected since Germany has not concluded a treaty with Poland concerning compensation, and the other shareholders in consequence will get no compensation, and since a shareholder in a going concern according to the ordinary interpretation of company law cannot raise any claim against third party in respect of loss caused to the company. A claim of this kind, discussed during the Danish-Polish compensation negotiations, as a matter of fact, was also rejected by Poland.

Ex. 2: An American citizen owns shares in a Swiss company (company II) which owns property that has been nationalized in Jugoslavia.

Both Switzerland and the United States have concluded treaties with Jugoslavia concerning payment of compensation for nationalized property, but the treaties are different. Compensation to the United States is paid cash down in gold, whereas compensation to Switzerland is paid in instalments over a period of 10 years. In this case, too, it seems unnecessarily complicated and in conflict with the rules of company law, if the American citizen should be able to present a claim against Jugoslavia through the United States. On equal terms with the other shareholders in the Swiss company he may claim compensation through the Swiss Government, the compensation paid to Switzerland also comprising his claim.

The question consequently is whether it is in conformity with the view of the contracting states to draw the above unreasonable conclusions from the wording of the treaties and so understand the said treaty provision that compensation is payable in these cases to the state of nationality of the indirect owners.

This question probably must be answered in the negative.

The rule to the effect that indirect claims are also covered is found in lump-sum agreements and in the other forms of compensation agreements which, before they became effective, were superseded by lump-sum agreements. The said rule consequently cannot individually form a basis for claims as between the contracting states, since all compensationclaims in connection with acts of nationalization are finally settled by the payment of the lump-sum. The reason why the provision to the effect that all direct and indirect claims are covered by the agreement was included in the treaty may then be that it was desired thereby to give to the "balance receipt" contained in the lump-sum arrangement the widest possible scope, without all claims covered by the wide formulation having actually been recognized. This, e. g., was not the case in the Danish-Polish compensation negotiations, nor in the French-Polish negotiations, where the published list of compensated French interests only shows that compensation has been paid for property directly belonging to French physical or juridical persons.(1)

(1) *Journal officiel* of 11th November, 1951.

In reply to an inquiry the Swedish Ministry for Foreign Affairs unofficially stated that compensation for property that indirectly — through the medium of foreign companies — belonged to Swedish nationals has not been obtained by Sweden either. The British Foreign Office stated that the Foreign Compensation Commission (a British Commission distributing the compensation received) in some isolated cases has paid compensation for property nationalized in Jugoslavia and Czechoslovakia and belonging to companies having their situs in Switzerland but controlled by British shareholders. It is expressly emphasized that these compensation claims are not covered by the Swiss agreements (by reason of the British capital), and that it is not to be expected in future that such claims will be met.(1)

Lastly, it can be stated that in the agreement between Switzerland and Czechoslovakia of 18th December, 1946 (which was subsequently superseded by a global agreement) the provision concerning indirect ownership caused Czechoslovakia, by the supplementary protocol of 7th February, 1947,(2) art. 1, para. 4, being expressly exempted from payment of compensation for Swiss interests in German firms, since it was expected that such claims would be regulated at the coming peace conference with Germany. In this case, too, recognition of indirect ownership as a basis for compensation claims was rejected.

From what has been said here it will be clear that the recurrent provision in compensation treaties concerning indirect ownership has been of no practical importance. This provision, as a matter of fact, is not found in the latest global compensation agreements concluded between Norway and Bulgaria, 2nd December, 1955 and between Norway and Poland, 23rd December, 1955.

---

(1) The information provided by the British Foreign Office, however, does not show that Great Britain in fact obtained payment in respect of the said claims from Jugoslavia and Czechoslovakia, since the Commission distributes the amount received solely on the basis of English national law as laid down in the Foreign Compensation Act of 12th July, 1950. Even if Jugoslavia and Czechoslovakia had paid compensation for the said claims, it is still an open question whether in these cases there is a case of compensation to indirect owners. In Swiss law these companies do not have Swiss nationality, and the British control of the companies indicates that they are in reality British despite the fact that they are not registered in Great Britain, cf. what has been said above under B.

Concerning the Foreign Compensation Commission, see also Drucker, "Compensation for Nationalized Property: The British Practice," *A. J. I. L.*, vol. 49, (1955), p. 479 ff.

(2) Cf. Recueil officiel (1948) p. 547.

D. *At what point of time must the national ownership exist?*

This question receives a uniform answer in all the compensation treaties, namely, that the national ownership must exist both at the time of the measure of nationalization (normally, the day when the nationalization law comes into force) and also at the time when the compensation agreement is entered into.

This is in conformity with existing international law as regards compensation claims resulting from a breach of law, cf. in this connection the basis for discussion prepared for the Codification Conference in the Hague in 1930, where it is stated:

> "A state may not claim a pecuniary indemnity in respect of damage suffered by a private person in the territory of a foreign state unless the injured person was its national at the moment when the damage was caused and retains its nationality until the claim is decided ..."

Despite the fact that the problem was not discussed at the Conference, the above statement was regarded as an expression of international practice and of the view prevailing among the majority of those states which had replied to the questionnaire of the League of Nations on the subject.(1)

Certain compensation treaties, such as, for example, the Danish-Polish protocol I of 12th May, 1949, lay down the further rule that the property, to provide basis for compensation, must have been acquired before the outbreak of the War. This special rule was dictated by an interest in not having to compensate for property acquired with the aid of the enemy, or for the purpose of speculation in circumstances occasioned by the War, and it cannot influence the general rule of international law.

§ 18.

THE EXTENT OF COMPENSATION

A. *The determination of the amount of compensation.*

1. *Starting point: The compensation must be adequate.* The question of the amount of the compensation to be paid when a person is lawfully deprived of his property is answered in international legal theory to the effect that the compensation must be adequate or just, i. e. corresponding to the loss that results from

(1) Cf. Briggs, *op. cit.*, p. 733 and the quotations and references given there.

the dispossession.(1) Similar terms to describe the extent of the obligation of the nationalizing state to pay compensation are to be found in a number of treaties providing for compensation in the form which has been described above as individual compensation and not containing any specified methods of calculation.

The British-Polish agreement of 3rd January, 1946, thus contains in art. 3 the provision that "compensation shall be so assessed as to be adequate ..." The Swedish-Polish treaty of 28th February, 1947, lays down in art. 1, that Poland shall pay "just compensation". To this the Polish delegation in the final provision to the protocol made the reservation that after the above words there should be added the words "in accordance with the Polish legislation". In the Danish-Polish protocol I of 12th May, 1949, art. 11, it is stated that "the amounts of compensation shall be so fixed as to be adequate".

On the other hand in those treaties that provide for lump-sum compensation there are no statements as to the principles on which the amount of the compensation is to be fixed. Such statements are rightly taken to be superfluous as the exact amount of the compensation is fixed in the treaties. All the same the amount of lump-sum compensation gives some general guidance, since the determination of the lump-sum has often been made under reference to the principles that are laid down in the agreements concerning individual compensation which are superseded by the lump-sum compensation treaties.

The question then arises whether the compensation that is paid in pursuance of the agreements concluded is adequate or just in the sense in which these terms are traditionally understood in the literature and practice of international law, and in the sense, inter alia, expressed in the case Olson v. United States, where in the judgment given by the United States Supreme Court it is said:(2)

> "Just compensation includes all elements of value that inhere in the property, but it does not exceed market value fairly determined. The sum required to be paid the owner does not depend upon the uses to which he has devoted his land but is to be arrived at upon just consideration of all uses for which it is suitable. The highest and most profitable use for which the property is adaptable and needed or likely to be needed in the reasonable near future is to be considered, not necessarily as the measure of value, but to the full extent that the prospect of demand for such use affects the market value while the property is privately held."

(1) Cf. Friedman, *op. cit.*, p. 215, Hyde, "Compensation for Expropriation" *A. J. I. L.*, vol. 33, (1939), p. 112 and Whiteman, *op. cit.*, vol. II, p. 1386.

(2) 292, U. S. 246,255. Quoted from Hyde, *loc. cit.*, p. 110

2. *Practice.* It is not possible to give a clear answer to the question we are looking into without access to valuation of the items of property which form the basis on which the amount of compensation has been fixed. On the basis of available sources, however, it is possible to state that in connection with the agreement concluded 19th July, 1948, between the United States and Jugoslavia, in pursuance of which 17 million dollars were paid in compensation for nationalized property, it was announced in the House Committee on Foreign Affairs(1) that the settlement arrived at represented about 42·5 % of the amount originally claimed, and that the American government's legal advisers declared that the 17 million dollars would cover "the fair value of the claims".

According to the statements quoted by Schwarzenberger(2) the compensation that Poland was to pay to Great Britain amounted to about a third of the value of the British investments in Poland. The Czech compensation in pursuance of the treaty of 28th September, 1949 is also stated to amount to a third, while the amount of compensation fixed in the British-Jugoslav agreement of 23rd December, 1948, at £ 4·5 million is said to be half the value of the British investments. In the agreement of 11th April, 1951, British interests in the French nationalized gas and electricity industry obtained compensation to a value of 70 % of the amount of the private investments.

The compensation which Norway obtained by the compensation agreement with Poland of 23rd December, 1955, amounted to about 3·5 million Norwegian Kr., while the value of the nationalized property was estimated at 4·5 million Norwegian Kr.(3)

In view of these figures and statements, which might suggest that the compensation paid in pursuance of the compensation treaties was not adequate or just, the reservation must be made that the figures with which the compensation is compared often represent valuation of the claims made by the persons affected by the nationalization, and it is a well known fact even in national law that a claimant seldom underestimates his claim.

The guidance with regard to the determination of the amount of compensation which may be found in the existing treaty practice must therefore be looked for not in the figures given, but rather in the principles underlying the valuation under the negotiations be-

(1) HR 4406, 81st Cong. 1st. Sess. (1949) p. 7 and 18. Quoted from Rubin, *op. cit.*, p. 465.
(2) *British Property*, p. 307.
(3) Cf. *Stortingets prp.*, No. 103, (1955), p. 3.

tween the states, and it is against this background that we must examine whether the claimant is given a less favourable position than he would have had if nationalization had not taken place.

The principles which Poland invoked in negotiations, at any rate with Sweden(1) and Denmark,(2) are contained in art. 7 of the Polish nationalization law. It is stated there that in arriving at the amount of the compensation regard must be had to:

a) the general reduction in the Polish national wealth as a result of the War (estimated to be about 40 %),
b) the net value of the assets of the nationalized activity on the day the state takes over the same,(3)
c) the reduction of the value of the activity as a result of war damage and other losses occasioned by the War and the Occupation in the period from 1st September, 1939 up to the day the property is taken over by the state,
d) investments made after 1st September, 1939, and
e) special circumstances reducing the value of the activity (the duration of concessions and licences, etc.).

These principles — though in a somewhat different from — have by and large been invoked by all nationalizing states during negotiations with foreign states on the subject of compensation.

3. *Critical valuation.* It is not really possible to make any legal objections(4) to the above principles in determination of adequate compensation. Even in cases where nationalization did not take place, the assests of foreign nationals would be affected both by the general fall in the national wealth of the country where the investments were made as well as by war damage, etc. These are

(1) Cf. Treaty of 28th February, 1947. The Polish reservation, point 1.

(2) Cf. Treaty of 12th May, 1949, art. 7.

(3) The Italian Peace Treaty of 10th February, 1947, art. 78, para 4 (*U.N., Treaty Series*, vol. 49, p. 161) expresses the principle that compensation for dispossession of property shall be fixed on the basis of the value of the given property at the time of payment. This principle seems to conform very well to the aim of compensation, i. e. to restore a loss. But this view has not been adhered to logically, for it is added in the Peace Treaty that compensation shall only be paid to the value of two thirds of the repurchase value so determined. In this way the difference between this principle and the one stated in the Polish nationalization law practically speaking is elimated.

(4) But cf. the official Swedish view, as represented in the Swedish-Polish treaty of 28th February, 1947, where it is inserted in the text itself that the Swedish delegation considers the said principles to be contrary to international law.

risks which a person investing capital abroad should — and can — take into account when judging the expediency and economic safety of such investment.

The practical application of the above rules, however, will not always lead to adequate compensation.

It will, for example, be impossible in practice for the representatives of the claimant state to assess the net value of the property affected by nationalization, already because it has proved impossible to get acces to inspect the property.(1) Further, at the time when the value of the property is to be assessed there is probably no longer any free market for the nationalized property, and in the same way the exploitation and remunerativeness of the property, as a result of officially fixed wages, fixed prices for raw materials and finished goods, will be dependent on the action of the government that is to pay the compensation. Consequently there will not normally be any objective market value to guide the valuation.(2) Even in the cases where the nationalized property is a claim for money in the currency of the country, comprehensive monetary reforms and exchange regulations carried out in connection with or simultaneously with the nationalization, will often cause a depreciation or complete extinguishment of the value of such claims so far as foreign nationals are concerned.

The determination of the net value of the property at the time of nationalization — which is the actual basis of the fixation of the compensation — so in all essentials is left to the discretion of the government that is to pay the compensation, and by this very fact the adequacy of the amount of compensation can easily be eliminated.

On the background described here it is probably possible to say that the traditional principles of international law concerning the determination of compensation have not been set aside in the treaties so far concluded, although the discretionary element — which as a matter of fact is inherent in most calculations of compensation — as a result of the nature of the nationalized property and its extent, plays a predominant part.

---

(1) Cf. *The Norwegian Stortings prp.* No. 103, (1955) p. 3.

(2) Cf. also *Kunglig Majestäts prp.* No. 187 of 3rd March, 1950, concerning the practical difficulties encountered by the Swedish representatives in there attempt to determine compensation.

B. *The terms of payment.*

1. *Starting point: Compensation is to be paid promptly.* In close connection with the determination of the amount of the compensation is the question whether payment is to be made in immediate cash or whether the compensation is to be paid by instalments.(1) The traditional view in international law in connection with expropriation of foreign property is that the payment of compensation is to be made, preferably in advance, and at any rate promptly.

This rule, that aims at restricting expropriation to cases where the interest of the state in taking over the property is so great that advance or prompt compensation is not by comparison considered a heavy economic disposition, as indicated earlier cannot be applied to nationalization of foreign property.

If the nationalized property is of any substantial value it will be impossible for any state to meet a claim for adequate compensation, even with the above qualifications, if such compensation is to be paid cash.

2. *Practice.* The practical difficulties referred to above have caused that in practice the states — in case of nationalization have abandoned the traditional principle, and carried through payment by instalment. This principle of payment by instalment is used, moreover, in national law in those countries where compensation is paid also in respect of the nationalization of the property of nationals. It may thus be mentioned by way of example that in Great Britain and in France compensation has been paid in the form of national bonds redeemable over a period of years.

The principle of payment by instalment is similarly applied in all effective compensation agreements, in case where compensation is paid to the individual claimants in governments bonds(2) as well as in case of global compensation.

However, in one isolated case the United States Government did protest against the instalment principle. In a Note dated 28th Au-

(1) "The global sum an the period of payment are directly dependent upon one another. To the extent to which the period of payment is extended, the Swedish shareholder must claim a higher global sum, and, conversely, he would be disposed to accept a lower figure if the period of payment were to be shorter. This state of affairs is connected with the fact that no interest is stipulated in the agreement ..." *Kunglig Majestäts prp.*, No. 187, (1950), p. 17.

(2) Cf. the agreements between France and Belgium of 18th February, 1949, and between France and Switzerland, of 21st November, 1949.

gust, 1953, to Guatemala, on the occasion of the expropriation of certain territories belonging to the American-owned United Fruit Company, it is stated:

> "Payment in bonds maturing in 25 years, with interest at 3 per cent per annum, and of uncertain market value, is scarcely to be regarded as either prompt or effective payment. Many of the holders will realize little on the bonds in the course of their lives.
> The offer of payment in bonds under all circumstances is not of a nature to offer 'the full guarantee and protection' of either the law of Guatemala or of the law of nations ..."(1)

The protest appears to have its particular justification in the unduly poore conditions, i. e., low rate of interest, long-term currency, variations in the rate of exchange, etc., offered by Guatemala.

As to the number of instalments and the extent of the period of payment it is not easy on the basis of existing treaty practice to lay down any general rule, since the period of payment in the said treaties ranges from 3 to 17 years. This period will depend on the individual circumstances, including the extent of the nationalized property, the amount of compensation, the expectations of future commercial relations, etc.

In some of the treaties it has been agreed that the compensation shall be paid in a fairly large amount cash and the remainder spread over a number of years. This is the case in the treaties between Great Britain and Jugoslavia, 23rd December, 1948, Switzerland and Czechoslovakia, 22nd December, 1949, Switzerland and Roumania, 3rd August, 1951, Switzerland and Bulgaria, 26th November, 1954, and Norway and Bulgaria, 2nd December, 1955. In these cases, as well as in those where the whole amount of the compensation was paid cash, cf. the agreements between the United States and Jugoslavia, 19th July, 1948, and between Poland and Norway, 23rd December, 1955, there was, however, the special feature that the said cash amounts could be set off against assets available in the countries that were to receive compensation. The provisions of these treaties as to terms of payment cannot, therefore, be considered of a general significance.

3. *Critical valuation.* The practice examined above shows that states in general regard payment by instalment satisfactory settlement of claims for compensation for nationalization. This form of payment will meet the interest of both states involved. The nationalizing state can carry out the necessary nationalization without

(1) Cf. *Dep. St. Bul.*, vol. 29, (1953), p. 359.

fearing exorbitant international claims being presented for immediate settlement, and without the risk of trade relations, etc. being broken off because the nationalizing state has not at its disposal the large sums demanded to make immediate cash payment. On the other hand, the disadvantage caused by the instalment system to the state entitled to compensation can be substantially reduced if the amount of compensation is increased in proportion to the length of the period of payment.

The postponement of the time of payment brought about through the principle of payment by instalment consequently is the result which international practice among states — in contrast to La Pradelle(1) — has arrived at due to the usually very great value of the nationalized property.

C. *The nature of the compensation.*

1. *Starting point: The compensation shall be effective.* The prevalent lack of convertible currency after the Second World War, together with the currency restrictions imposed in practically speaking all nationalizing countries, as well as inflationary trends, have entailed certain currency problems in connection with the payment of compensation to foreign nationals. The solution of these problems — in the same way as the determination of the amount of compensation and the terms of payment — is a decisive factor in determining the extent of the compensation.

The problems arise in connection with the choice between the following possibilities:

a) Payment in the currency of the nationalizing state.
b) Payment in the currency of the claimant state.
c) Payment in the convertible currency of a third state.

The theoretical solution of the currency problems,(2) i. e., making the compensation effective, must take its starting point in the object of the compensation, i. e. to ensure to the claimant financial indemnity so that his financial position remains unaffected by the nationalization.

The consequence of this appears to be that payment ought to be made in the currency of the state in which the nationalized property was situated at the time of the nationalization.

---

(1) Cf. *supra* p. 77.
(2) Cf. Bindschedler, *op. cit.*, p. 56.

This theoretical solution is supported by the fact that the investor voluntarily placed his capital in the nationalizing state and must therefore have been able to foresee the possibility of the losses which inflation and currency restrictions etc. in the country of investment might cause him. The value of the property is determined precisely by the economic opportunities in that country in which the property is located, and it therefore seems reasonable that the compensation, computed on the basis of the value of the property, should suffer the same fate. Compensation in convertible currency, whether that of the claimant state or the currency of a third state, or merely compensation in the non-convertible currency of the claimant state, may possibly mean a substantial financial advantage for the person affected by the nationalization compared with the status of foreign owners of, or shareholders in, non-nationalized activities. These latter probably have no opportunity of getting their capital out of the country of investment. Further, and this is very significant in practice, the state liable to pay compensation will but rarely have at its disposal currency other than its own for the purpose of payment of compensation.(1)

The view that the compensation payment for foreign property shall be made in the currency of the country in which the property is situated is, moreover, recognized in the peace treaty with Italy concluded 10th February, 1947, art. 78 para 4,(2) where it is laid down that compensation in respect of property that formerly belonged to nationals of the United Nations shall be paid "... in lire to the extent of two-thirds of the sum necessary, at the day of payment, to purchase similar property or to make good the loss received". Similar provisions are included in the peace treaties with Bulgaria, of the same date, in art. 23, para 4 (payment in levas),(3) with Hungary in art. 26, para 4 (»in Hungarian currency«)(4) and with Roumania in art. 24, para 4 (in lei).(5)

Despite all that has been said here, payment in the currency of the nationalizing state must nevertheless be rejected,(6) since the back-

---

(1) Cf. for example, the Polish Government's Note of 30th April, 1946, to the United States Government, where it is stated inter alia: "In order to achieve ... that compensation to citizens of the United States be effected in a manner which would permit an exchange of the amounts paid for dollars in the shortest possible time, the dollar reserves of Poland must first be substantially increased ..." *Dep. St. Bul.*, vol. 15, (1946), p. 653.

(2) *U.N., Treaty Series*, vol. 49, p. 161.

(3) *U.N., Treaty Series*, vol. 41, p. 68.

(4) *U.N., Treaty Series*, vol. 41, p. 192.

(5) *U.N., Treaty Series*, vol. 42, p. 52.

(6) Friedman takes a different view, *op. cit.*, p. 218—219.

ground for the arguments quoted does not exist in the case of nationalization.

The investments were in many cases made at a time when the currency of the country of investment was convertible, and when the currency restrictions in force to-day were phenomena as yet unknown. The advantage that there might possibly be in having the compensation paid in the currency of the claimant state or in free convertible currency probably will not in practice — considering the amounts paid — be regarded as any enrichment compared with the opportunities of foreign nationals, whose property is not affected by the nationalization.

Further, however — and this is decisive — payment in the currency of the nationalizing state will seldom constitute any redress to the person entitled to compensation, for he will normally be precluded from reinvestment in the same or similar kinds of activities in that country. His possibility of using the compensation received in the nationalizing country will as often as not — though not always — be limited to the purchase of government bonds. Consequently the practice adopted in the said peace treaties cannot be of any guidance, either, in the solution of this problem, since the provisions appear to imply that the person receiving compensation can use the money received for the purchase of property corresponding to the property lost.

The conclusion from these views must be that in order to be effective the compensation must be paid in a currency other than that of the nationalizing state in case the nationalizing state should be hostile to foreign investment by precluding such investment or restricting it to so limited spheres that reinvestment is without practical significance. This must at any rate hold good where investments in the now nationalized property was at the time made in foreign currency.

2. *Practice.* The above result indeed appears to be recognized in treaty practice.

The treaty concluded between Sweden and Poland, 28th February, 1947, thus provides in art. 5, that the following principles shall be the basis of the computation of compensation:

"a) Where Swedish currency is directly invested in Poland by Swedish physical and juridical persons, the compensation shall be paid in Swedish Kronor for a similar proportion of the compensation accorded as the proportion which the amount of directly invested Swedish currency forms in relation to the total amount invested. The following shall be regarded as directly invested Swedish Kronor:

1) Investments or credits originating through the transfer direct to Poland of Swedish currency or Swedish goods.
2) Investments or credits originating through the transfer direct to Poland of other currencies at a time when Polish zlotys could be freely converted into Swedish Kronor.
3) Reinvestments in Polish zlotys at a time when Polish zlotys were freely convertible into Swedish Kronor."

The treaty concluded between Great Britain and Poland, 24th January, 1948, contains in art. 13 a provision to the effect that the compensation securities which are to be paid to British recipients of compensation shall be sterling securities in those cases where the investment had been made in the following ways:

"(i) Investment made by transferring sterling to Poland.
(ii) Investment made by transferring other currency to Poland at a time when such currency was convertible into sterling.
(iii) Accumulation or reinvestment in Poland of undistributed profits in zlotys at a time when the zloty was convertible into sterling.
(iv) Introduction into the undertaking of any items of property which may be agreed to constitute an investment of capital.
(v) Rendering, in pursuance of a contractual obligation of any substantial technical or economic assistance or other services which, after discussion by the Mixed Commission may be agreed to constitute an investment of capital".

In other cases, for example, where investment had been made in the form of Polish currency, the compensation is to be paid in zloty securities.

Such detailed provisions do not occur in the Danish-Polish protocol of 12th May, 1949, for it is simply stated in art. 11 that the adequate payment "shall be paid effectively, and that negotiations concerning the transfer of the compensation sum to Denmark shall take place between the two governments". The problem of payment was as a matter of fact settled in connection with the agreement on global compensation treaty cf. infra.

By the compensation treaties, e. g., with Belgium, 18th February, 1949, and Switzerland, 21st November, 1949, France carried through an arrangement to the effect that the compensation was to be paid in government stock in French francs, but subject to a dollar clause providing that the French government guarantees a fixed dollar value of the franc specified in the treaties. The interest yield of the stock and the principal money when payed can be used by the recipient for reinvestment in France.

The other agreements on individual compensation do not contain any regulations as to the currency in which payment is to be effected.(1)

It appears, however, as if the currency problem in connection with the payment of compensation discussed here has solved itself. The treaty practice of more recent years, which abandons the principle of individual compensation in favour of the principle of global compensation contains no indication of the difficulties with which the draftsmen of the above treaties were obviously confronted. The payment of lump-sum compensation is effected as a rule in merchandise or by the release of capital that has been frozen in the claimant state. The physical or juridical persons who are entitled to compensation will consequently receive their compensation in their national currency. This solution as a matter of fact is in good accordance with the views stated above as based upon the merits of the problem.

In one isolated case the global sum in part was paid in the currency of the nationalizing state. By the treaty between Switzerland and Hungary, 19th July, 1950, Hungary undertook to pay as part of the global sum 3,740,029 forint. It was, however, expressly agreed that this sum should be convertible. This satisfies the requirements of international law concerning effective payment.

---

(1) Schwarzenberger says, however, in *British Property*, p. 306, that Mexico fulfilled its compensation obligation in pursuance of the agreements of 7th February, 1946, with Great Britain and Holland by paying the compensation sums in USA dollars.

APPENDIX A.

SURVEY OF THE COMPENSATION TREATIES REFERRED TO (CHRONOLOGICAL)(1)

Treaty	Form(2)	Amount and Currency	Terms of payment
Sweden — Soviet Russia 30. 5. 1941 and 7. 10. 1946	G	19,580,000 Sw. Kr.	Instalments
U. S. A. — Mexico 7. 2. 1946	II	29,137,700 $	Instalments over 4 years
Great Britain — Mexico 7. 2. 1946	II	$	Instalments
Holland — Mexico 7. 2. 1946	II	$	
U. S. A. — Poland 24. 4. 1946	U		
Sweden — Hungary 26. 7. 1946	U		
U. S. A. — Czechoslovakia 14. 11. 1946	U		
Switzerland — Czechoslovakia 18. 12. 1946	DI		

(1) The details in the above survey are taken in the main from collections of treaties, etc. accessible to the public.

(2) U = Unspecified agreement on compensation.
DI = Direct individual compensation.
II = Indirect individual compensation.
G = Global compensation.

Treaty	Form	Amount and Currency	Terms of payment
U. S. A. — Poland 27. 12. 1946	II		
Sweden — Poland 28. 2. 1947	DI		
Sweden — Czechoslovakia 15. 3. 1947	U		
Belgium — Czechoslovakia 19. 3. 1947	DI		
Sweden — Jugoslavia 12. 4. 1947	G		
Denmark — Poland 5. 12. 1947	U		
Great Britain — Poland 24. 1. 1948	DI		
Norway — Poland 4. 2. 1948	U		
France — Poland 19. 7. 1948	G	Value of 3·8 mill. tons of coal	2 mill. tons in 15 years. The remainder to be arranged.
U. S. A. — Jugoslavia 19. 7. 1948	G	17,000,000 $	Cash set off against gold account
France — Czechoslovakia 6. 8. 1948	DI		

Treaty	Form	Amount and Currency	Terms of payment
Switzerland — Jugoslavia 27. 9. 1948	G	75,000,000 Sw. Frcs.	Instalments over 10 years
Great Britain — Jugoslavia 23. 12. 1948	G	4,500,000 £	10 % set off against cash. Remainder over 7½ years
Great Britain — Poland 14. 1. 1949	G	Final sum not fixed.	
Belgium — France 18. 2. 1949	DI		
Denmark — Poland 12. 5. 1949	II		
Italy — Jugoslavia 23. 5. 1949	II		
Switzerland — Poland 25. 6. 1949	G	53,500,000 Sw. Frcs.	Instalments over 13 years
Great Britain — Czechoslovakia 28. 9. 1949	G	8,000,000 £	Instalments over 9 years
Holland — Czechoslovakia 4. 11. 1949	DI		
Sweden — Poland 16. 11. 1949	G	116,000,000 Sw. Kr.	Instalments over 17 years
Switzerland — France 21. 11. 1949	DI		

Treaty	Form	Amount and Currency	Terms of payment
Switzerland — Czechoslovakia 22. 12. 1949	G	71,000,000 Sw. Frcs.	28 mill. set off against cash. Remainder over 10 years
Turkey — Jugoslavia 5. 1. 1950	II		
France — Czechoslovakia 2. 6. 1950	G	4,200 mill. Fr. Frcs.	Instalments over 10 years
France — Hungary 12. 6. 1950	G	(1)	Instalments(1)
Switzerland — Hungary 19. 7. 1950	G	29,981,000 Sw. Frcs. + 3,740,029 forint (convertible).	Instalments over 10 years
Sweden — Hungary 31. 3. 1951	G	33,170,000 Sw. Kr.	Instalments over 3-13 years depending upon the nature of the claim
Great Britain — France 11. 4. 1951	DI		
France — Jugoslavia 14. 4. 1951	G	Value of 15,000,000 $ paid in Fr. Frcs.	Instalments over 10 years

(1) It has not been possible to find out the amount of the global sum nor of the instalments. The instalments, which are fixed for each year, in 1954 amounted to 64,000,000 Fr. frc.

Treaty	Form	Amount and Currency	Terms of payment
Switzerland — Roumania 3. 8. 1951	G	42,500,000 Sw. Frs.	25·5 mill. set off against cash. Remainder over 8 years
Belgium — Czechoslovakia 30. 9. 1952	G	425,000,000 Belg. Frcs.	Further agreement to be negotiated.
Denmark — Poland 26. 2. 1953	G	5,700,000 Danish Kr.	Instalments over 15 years
Great Britain — Poland 11. 11. 1954	G	5,465,000 £	Instalments over 12 years — period possibly to be extended.
Switzerland — Bulgaria 26. 11. 1954	G	7,500,000 Sw. Frcs.	2·5 mill. set off against cash. Remainder over 10 years
Belgium/ Luxembourg — Hungary 1. 2. 1955	G	95,000,000 Belg. Frcs.	Instalments over 10 years
Great Britain — Bulgaria 20. 9. 1955	G	400,000 £	Instalments dependent on Bulgarian exports.
Norway — Bulgaria 2. 12. 1955	G	175,000 N. Kr.	34,562 cash. The remainder paid by instalments relative to Bulgarian exports
Norway — Poland 23. 12. 1955	G	About 3-3·5 million N. Kr.	Sett off against cash

APPENDIX B.

SURVEY OF THE FORMS OF COMPENSATION(1)

A. Unspecified agreements concerning compensation.

U. S. A. — Poland 24. 4. 1946
Sweden — Hungary 26. 7. 1946
U. S. A. — Czechoslovakia 14. 11. 1946
Sweden — Czechoslovakia 15. 3. 1947
Denmark — Poland 5. 12. 1947
Norway — Poland 4. 2. 1948

B. Agreements concerning direct individuel compensation.

Switzerland — Czechoslovakia 18. 12. 1946
Sweden — Poland 28. 2. 1947
Belgium — Czechoslovakia 19. 3. 1947
Great Britain — Poland 24. 1. 1948
France — Czechoslovakia 6. 8. 1948
Belgium — France 18. 2. 1949
Holland — Czechoslovakia 4. 11. 1949
Switzerland — France 21. 11. 1949
Great Britain — France 11. 4. 1951

C. Agreements concerning indirect individuel compensation.

U. S. A. — Mexico 29. 9. 1943
Great Britain — Mexico 7. 2. 1946
Holland — Mexico 7. 2. 1946
U. S. A. — Poland 27. 12. 1946
Denmark — Poland 12. 5. 1949
Italy — Jugoslavia 23. 5. 1949(2)
Turkey — Jugoslavia 5. 1. 1950(2)

---

(1) The treaties in italics are those where no compensation has been paid in pursuance of them, either because when they were concluded they were already intended to be provisional, or because the system of compensation laid down in the treaty has proved in practice to be unworkable, cf. § 15.

(2) It has not been possible to find out whether in pursuance of these treaties compensation has been paid out.

D. Agreements concerning global compensation.

Sweden — Soviet Russia 30. 5. 1941
Sweden — Jugoslavia 12. 4. 1947
France — Poland 19. 3. 1948
U. S. A. — Jugoslavia 19. 7. 1948
Switzerland — Jugoslavia 27. 9. 1948
Great Britain — Jugoslavia 23. 12. 1948
Great Britain — Poland 14. 1. 1949
Switzerland — Poland 25. 6. 1949
Great Britain — Czechoslovakia 28. 9. 1949
Sweden — Poland 16. 11. 1949
Switzerland — Czechoslovakia 22. 12. 1949
France — Czechoslovakia 2. 6. 1950
France — Hungary 12. 6. 1950
Switzerland — Hungary 19. 7. 1950
Sweden — Hungary 31. 3. 1951
France — Jugoslavia 14. 4. 1951
Switzerland — Roumania 3. 8. 1951
Belgium — Czechoslovakia 30. 9. 1952
Denmark — Poland 26. 2. 1953
Great Britain — Poland 11. 11. 1954
Switzerland — Bulgaria 26. 11. 1954
Belgium/Luxembourg — Hungary 1. 2. 1955
Great Britain — Bulgaria 20. 9. 1955
Norway — Bulgaria 2. 12. 1955
Norway — Poland 23. 12. 1955.

LITERATURE CITED AND ABBREVIATIONS

A. J. I. L.: American Journal of International Law.

ANDERSEN, POUL: Dansk Statsforfatningsret, vol. 1, (1954).

ANDERSON, CHARLES: "Title to Confiscated Property", A. J. I. L., vol 20, (1926), p. 528.

ANNUAIRE: Annuaire de l'Institut de droit international.

ANZILOTTI, D.: Cours de droit international (1929).

BINDSCHEDLER, R. L.: Verstaatlichungsmassnahmen und Entschädigungspflicht nach Völkerrecht (1950).

BORCHARD, EDWIN M.: The Diplomatic Protection of Citizens Abroad (1916).

BRIGGS, HERBERT W.: The Law of Nations (1953).

BRUCKER, ALFRED: "Compensation for Nationalized British Property: British Practice", A. J. I. L., vol. 49, (1955), p. 477.

BULLINGTON, JOHN P.: "Problems of International Law in the Mexican Constitution of 1917", A. J. I. L., vol. 21, (1927), p. 685.

B. Y. I. L.: British Year Book of International Law.

CASTEL, G.: "Immunity of a Foreign State from Execution: French Practice", A. J. I. L., vol. 46, (1952), p. 520.

CHENG: "International Law in the United Nations", Year Book of World Affairs, (1954).

DEP. ST. BUL.: Departement of State Bulletin.

DICKENS, POUL D. and REEVES, WILL HARVEY: "Foreign Investments", Political Science Quarterly, (1949), p. 211.

DOMAN, N. R.: "Postwar Nationalization of Foreign Property in Europe", Columbia Law Review, vol. 48, (1948), p. 1125.

DUUN, F. S.: Protection of Nationals (1932).

FACHIRI, ALEX P.: "Expropriation and International Law", B. Y. I. L., vol. 6, (1925), p. 139.

FAWCETT, J. E. S.: "Some Foreign effects of Nationalization of Property", B. Y. I. L., vol. 27, (1950), p. 355.

FISCHER-WILLIAMS, JOHN: "International Law and the Property of Aliens", B. Y. I. L., vol. 9, (1928), p. 1.

FORD, ALAN W.: The Anglo-Iranian Oil Dispute 1951—1952 (1954).

FRIEDMAN, S.: Expropriation in International Law (1953).

GAITHER, ROSCOE, B.: Expropriation in Mexico, The facts and the Law (1940).

GOLDBERGER, LEON og METZGER, LAURE: "The Polish Nationalization Law". Dep. St. Bul., vol. 15, (1946), p. 651.

HACKWORTH, G. H.: Digest on International Law, vol. I-V (1940—1944).

HEILLRONER, ROBERT L.: "Labour Unrest in the British Nationalized Sector", Social Research, vol. 19, (1952), p. 61.

HYDE, CHARLES CHENEY: International Law, Chiefly as Interpreted and Applied by the United States, vol. I-III (1947).

HYDE, CHARLES CHENEY: "Compensation for Expropriation", A. J. I. L., vol. 33, (1939), p. 108.

I. C. J.: International Court of Justice.

Indstilling fra Socialiseringskomiteen angående socialiseringsspørgsmålet i almindelighed med bilag (1924).

JONES, J. MERVYN: "Claims on Behalf of Nationals who are Shareholders in Foreign Companies", B. Y. I. L. vol 26, (1949), p. 225.

JOSEPH, F. M.: International Aspects of Nationalization (1954).

KAECKENBEECK, G.: "The Protection of Vested Rights in International Law", B. Y. I. L., vol. 17, (1936), p. 2.

KELSEN, HANS: Principles of International Law (1952).

KRENCHEL, H. B.: Håndbog i dansk Aktieret (1954).

KUNGL. MAJ:TS PRP.: Kunglig Majestäts proposition, Riksdagens Protokoll.

LA PRADELLE, A. DE: "Les effects internationaux des nationalisations", Annuaire, vol. 43 I (1950), p. 42.

LARSEN, EGON: Tvungen ejendomsafståelse (1940).

LEONIDAN, A.: "Shame Nationalization of the British Iron and Steel Industry", New Times, (1948), nr. 28, p. 4.

LOUIS-LUCAS, PIERE: "Remarques relatives a la determination de la nationalité des societes", La Semaine Juridique (1953), p. 1104.

MANN, F. A.: "Zum Problem der Staatsangehörigkeit der juristischen Person", Festschrift für Martin Wolf (1952), p. 271.

MINC, HILARY: The Nationalization of Industri in Poland (1946).

MOODIE, A.: "Agrarian Reforms in East Central Europe", Yearbook of World Affairs, (1954), p. 242.

MOORE, JOHN BASSET: Digest of International Law, vol. I-VIII (1906).

MYERS, MARGARET G.: "The Nationalization of Banks in France", Political Science Quarterly, (1949), p. 189.

NIEMEYER, GERHART: Law without Force (1941).

N. T. I. R.: Nordisk Tidsskrift for International Ret, Acta Scandinavica juris gentium.

OATMAN, MIRIAM E.: "The Nationalization Program in Czechoslovakia", Dep. St. Bul., vol. 15, (1946), p. 1028.

ODEVALL, BENGT: Globalersättning för ekonomiska intressen i utlandet", N. T. I. R., vol. 24, (1954), p. 16.

OPPENHEIM — LAUTERPACHT: International Law, vol. 1, (1947).

P. C. I. J.: Permanent Court of International Justice.

RECUEIL OFFICIEL: Recueil officiel des lois et ordonnances de la Confédération suisse.

REVIEW: Review of Economic Conditions in the Middle East, U.N. Secretariat, Departement of Economic Affairs (1951).

R.I.A.A.: Report of International Arbitral Awards, United Nation, vol. I-III (1948—1949).

ROBINSON, NEHEMIA: "Reparations and Restitution in International Law", The Jewish Yearbook of International Law, (1948) p. 186.

ROSS, ALF & ANDERSEN, ERNST: Dansk Statsforfatningsret II (1948).

ROSS, ALF: Textbook of International Law (1946).

ROSS, ALF & FOIGHEL, ISI: Studiebog i Folkeret (1954).

RUBIN, SEYMOUR J.: "Nationalization and Compensation, A Comparative Approach", The University of Chicago Law Review, vol. 17, (1949—1950).

SCAMMEL, E.H.: "Nationalization in legal Perspective", Current Legal Problems, vol. 5, (1952), p. 30.

SCELLE, GEORGES: Précis de droit de gens, vol. II (1934).

SCHWARZENBERGER, GEORG: International Law, vol. I (1945).

SCHWARZENBERGER, GEORG: "British Property Abroad", Current Legal Problems, vol. 5, (1952), p. 296.

SEIDL-HOHENVELDERN, IGNAZ: Internationales Konfiskations- und Enteignungsrecht (1952).

SHAWCROSS, HARTLEY: Some Problems of Nationalization (1954).

STERNTHAL, ADOLF: "The Structure of Nationalized Enterprises in France", Political Science Quarterly (1952), p. 57.

STRUPP, KARL: Das völkerrechtliche Delikt (1920).

S.Ö.: Sveriges överenskommelser med främmede makter. (Swedish Treaty Series).

SØRENSEN, MAX: International Organisation (1952).

TOBIN, IRWIN M.: "Nationalization in Great Britain — First Year", Dep. St. Bul., vol. 15, (1946), p. 615.

T.S.: British Treaty Series.

U.f.R.: Ugeskrift for Retsvæsen. (Danish Law Review).

U.N. TREATY SERIES: United Nations Treaty Series.

WALKER, G.J.: The Transport Act 1947, Economic Journal, vol. 58, (1948), p. 11.

VERDROSS, ALFRED VON: Völkerrecht (1937).

WHITEMAN, MARJORIE M.: Damages in International Law, vol. I-III, (1932).

WOOLSEY, L.H.: "Expropriation of Oil Properties in Mexico", A.J.I.L., vol. 32, (1938), p. 519.

YEAR BOOK: Year Book of the United Nations (1952).